HOW NOT TO MAKE
IT IN HOLLYWOOD

David Hern

ISBN: 979-8-218-37231-6

Edited by Meghan McEnery
Original Cover Art and Design by Paul Harrod

For "The Unknown Actor"

Contents

INTRO

How many times have you been watching television and heard someone say…

"Believe in your dreams. Find that thing in life that you love doing more than anything else in the world. Now, find a way to earn a living doing it and you'll never work a day in your life. Envision yourself successful in that role and follow through on it. If you can imagine it, you can make it a reality. Stay your course and don't listen to all the naysayers or negative people. Don't let them destroy your dreams. They are people too afraid to take a risk on making their dreams come true."

Sounds pretty good, doesn't it? Well, I sure believed it. All of it.

I completely bought into the spirituality of success through visualization. Especially the part about believing in your dreams. Because man, did I ever have some dreams. Vivid dreams. Many, many exciting, complex, detailed dreams involving me on the set of a picture that I had written and was also playing a supporting role in. In the middle of a one-off story conference between myself, the director, and the lead actress. Or eating lunch with the director of photography, talking about the next set-up. Or finally getting a great take of the hardest bit of physical comedy. Or watching the rushes in a really nice screening room on a big studio lot. Or. Or. Or. I believed in my dreams all day and night. I believed in them as my hair went grey.

If you go to the "Theatre" section of your bookstore, online or at your mall, you will find books with titles like *The Actor's Handbook, Essentials for a Career in Film and Television, The Do's and Don'ts of Hollywood.* These books are chock-full of practical advice and showbiz tidbits that use a lot of industry lingo. You will find most contain points like the following:

1. "<u>Get a day job.</u> You can't pursue a career without a roof over your head and food on the table. Plus, you need to be able to afford expenses like transportation to and from auditions."

2. "<u>Get your picture and resume done right.</u> Find a reputable photographer for your headshot, one that should look as much like you do in natural light. And on your resume, be sure to put your biggest credits at the top."

3. "<u>Continue to study your craft.</u> Find an acting coach or class that meets regularly for scene work, performance, and critique. Like a musician practicing their instrument, nothing helps your confidence level quite like ongoing rehearsal and scene work."

4. "<u>Look for an agent.</u>"

These books, at least for me, were annoyingly vague on details. They all sounded perfectly reasonable and encouraging, which feels good when you're struggling. What they do *not* contain are the how's and why's. The facts about the industry and its structures. The truths of what is involved in pursuing an actual career.

For a decade, I did everything technically "right." Got the day job, the pix/res, the classes going, and the search for an agent underway. In fact, I became a dedicated, nonstop industry machine. Despite whatever day job I had, every single day I would do at least one thing to further my career: mail off a script, call an agent, edit my audition reel, go to rehearsal for a showcase, do some writing on the next project. I was egged on by friends who kept saying things like, "Jesus, Dave, you're relentless; something's bound to break just on the numbers."

I was always told a career in showbiz takes "a combination of talent, perseverance, and luck." But every time I heard that, I would always think, well, I have plenty of the first two. When does the third kick in? I thought I was being reasonable, too. I had a single, solitary goal. Freedom from day jobs. That was it. I wanted to see if I could actually earn enough to sustain myself, nothing more or less. I just wanted out of the prison of day jobs. I believed my goals were attainable. I envisioned myself a successful middle-tier character actor, like my coaches, who's work I admired and wished to emulate. They worked enough to survive off their residuals but could still retain anonymity and go about their lives. I thought, well, that's reasonable, isn't it? Not aiming too high am I, shooting for third tier-dom?

I learned that Hollywood is a huge, impenetrable castle surrounded by a very wide and deep moat filled with slimy, predatory creatures. The only way in is if someone already on the inside lets down a drawbridge and allows you to enter. Nobody really lives in the castle and even the people who get inside can only stay for a limited period. Eventually, their time ends. So that makes the castle itself a bit of a mirage. A place everyone wants to get into but doesn't really exist. I also learned that they don't just let you act because you want to and you're good at it. You can't just walk up and say, "Hi, I would like to be a well-paid actor please."

In my handful of reasons for writing this book, probably the biggest one was that I wish there had been such a book available when I first landed in Hollywood. I could have used some guidance. During my wanderings, I spent a lot of time being misled. I fell for a lot of scams, made a lot of mistakes, and believed a lot of dubious wisdoms coming from questionable people. So, this is a book for actors who do all kinds of ridiculous things in the name of their careers. If nothing else, I figure it might help other actors avoid some of the many pitfalls I pit-fell into. Maybe save you a few bucks as well. Ideally, if blind luck is truly with you, you will smoothly bypass every one of the roadblocks I ran into. Even so, learning how to fail is one of the best things I or anyone else could impart to you. Having a measure of grace and resilience in that area will always come in handy regardless of the ups and downs of your life or career. I'm offering a pat on the back along the way.

This isn't a "tell-all" book either, since that connotes spilling-the-beans on somebody. The only *untrue* thing in this book is the occasional name, which I have fictionalized when necessary to avoid pissing off—or for that matter—pleasing anyone. I also include a smattering of things that might sound like advice but are really meant to be taken with a grain of your own personal seasoned salt. So, where to start?

To amuse myself, I started this book by writing my book jacket biography:

"**David Hern** is a failed actor and writer, full of bitterness and resentment for not being able to realize lifelong creative dreams in an industry geared for profit and unsympathetic toward art and artists. He pissed away a perfectly good college education and blew whatever money he earned on furthering his delusions. In the process, he lost decades of struggle for reasons he is still not clear on. He lives and works in Northern California where he continues to write and act despite all the evidence."

When the young Oscar winner holds the statue above his head and says, "To all the struggling actors out there, I just want to say, if I can make it, you can too! I'm living proof!" I would beg to differ on that. Serendipity is real, happenstance is real and certain fortunate confluences do indeed propel some people forward, but those instances are not reliable on the roulette wheel. Anecdotal evidence does not a case make. Ask any lawyer.

Also, "making it" is an illusion too, just like the pictures on the screen. Bette Davis famously had to take out a full-page ad in *Daily Variety* reminding the world, and the industry in particular, that she was still alive and available for work. And she was already a star. Gene Wilder was once quoted saying, "Be careful what you want, because you might get it." Actors are largely expendable. When an actor dies, it doesn't create a job opening.

Oh, I guess I should mention that reality television has blurred many lines. Used to be that the only people on TV or in movies were actors. Now, people can become celebrities just for being their stupid, selfish, loud-mouthed selves in contrived situations. Then, sometimes they put those people on TV or in movies, whether they can act or not. Sometimes they become president. I really can't speak to any of this. So, let's get all of that out of the way as this is a book for actors. Or anyone who feels like they're acting their way through life.

Welcome and thanks for reading. Let's have some fun.

AGENTS

Actors need agents. Sorry about that. I apologize. Really. Oh, how I wish this were not the case, but it is. When you don't have representation, you are forced into the endlessly humiliating business of constant self-promotion, something I admit I was never very good at. It's embarrassing. *"Yessireee Bob, I am just the kind of actor your agency needs! You don't want to miss out, so sign me today before it's too late!"*

If I had the gift of hype, I would have gone into advertising. I only knew how to write and act. So, naïvely, I approached the whole thing with the honest belief that I could make it on my talents alone. I thought, well, I'll just be *really* good, and somebody will notice. I never fully adjusted to the whole weird enterprise of selling your voice, your type, your physical self to someone else as an entertainment product to be marketed. That's what agents do. It's *their* job to do the hype, the sales, the negotiating and getting you up on auditions. That's why they get 10-15% of everything you earn. The more you work, the more they make. Your financial fates become intertwined.

So, one of the first things I did was pick up a current issue of *The Agents Directory* at a Hollywood bookstore. This monthly listing contained specific names of the various department heads of the franchised agencies with lengthy descriptions of who might be more "open to submissions" than others. It told you who worked for who, how long, etc. I marked up these things furiously with my own system of colored highlighters. It made these people feel more accessible and it gave me a plan of action. I hit each and every one, crossing them off as I went. Most told me to send a picture and resume, which I did (snail mail) along with a follow up call within a week, which was usually met with "leave a message." Sometimes I tried dropping them off with the goal of speaking directly with them. A few gave me a minute or two, nothing else. A couple of years later, after amassing enough film for a demo reel, the hunt continued now with demo reels in hand, like a peddler with my little sack of "me" for sale. One time, an agency that operated out of a renovated house told me, "Don't knock on the door. Just leave your demo out on the porch" which I did and learned on the follow-up, they had either lost it or never retrieved it.

After doing this for a year or so, one day the paradigm crumbled when in a different bookstore I saw something called an *Actor's Kit* which consisted of a copy of the directory PLUS pre-formatted mailing labels, envelopes, and everything you need to blitz the agencies. Basically, everything I had already done by hand, already done <u>for you</u>. Well, once I saw this, the dumb logic I had been operating on collapsed. Because if everyone is doing the same thing, that means agents know exactly what everyone is up to. They know what's filling up the mails. I need to make it clear that *none* of this yielded a thing, except a drawer full of letters. And I am *proud* to say that between writing and acting submissions, I have rejection letters from almost every MAJOR studio, agency, fellowship program, management group, and television producer in the entire Hollywood area. Thank you. Thank you so much. Please don't get up.

All right, let me just take a second to get this out of my system. For whatever reason, I could not get an agent for a bloodletting during my decade in Hollywood. If there is any group of people who I grew to detest and resent more over time, it would have to be agents. It's a horrible truth, but the very same people who can enable you to have a career can also *prevent* you from having one. Hollywood Agents—bane of my life. By the end of my stay, I was ready to boil them all in oil. Ahh, there. Ok, I feel so much better now.

Over the years, I exhausted every angle you can think of. I asked, bargained, begged, pleaded, cajoled, lied, wrote letters, and more to no avail. I dropped off tapes, mailed scripts, pictures, and resumes. I tried "reverse psychology," I made offers—"I'll tell you what, you don't have to sign me. Send me on three auditions. If I don't get any, I'll leave you alone. But if I get one, can we talk?" Nope. No thank you. Not. I kept looking for the sign on my back that says, "Do Not Represent." All the years of sitting locked outside, watching all the jobs go by, knowing that if I was out there auditioning, I would be getting gigs and working. But you can't take your shot if you're not allowed in the shooting gallery.

DAVID HERN

So, how *do* you get an agent? Well, here it is gang . . . the one you've been waiting for. The one you bought the book for. The answer to the age-old most mysterious question is actually very simple: *YOU DON'T*. An agent gets <u>you</u>. An agent must decide to represent you. It's a legal catch-22.

There are enough reasons for not signing you to fill an encyclopedia, so let's just have a look at the most popular ones, shall we? Let's start with the undisputed champion.

#1. *"We're not taking on any new clients right now."*

This one is as old as the business. The truth is, if a known, A-List actor was looking to change agents, they would all be clamoring for him, chasing through the jungle at four o'clock in the morning, stepping on each other's heads to get him signed immediately. In that sense, they are *always* taking on new clients. But what better way to get rid of somebody without sounding judgmental than by attributing it to some abstract company policy? When they want you, they will find you no matter where you are. When they don't, the silence is deafening.

One time, on one of my countless agent phone calls, after having been on the phone for hours, an agent's assistant threw this one at me and without thinking, I blurted out, *"Right.* You're telling me if Leonardo Di Caprio was looking for new representation, you wouldn't be interested because you're not taking on any new clients right now?" After a long pause, he just said, "Well, you're not Leonardo Di Caprio!" and hung up. Did you notice the other convenient thing about reason number one? "Right now," is a permanent condition. It will always be right now. So, does that mean they will never sign another client? Maybe. Or maybe just not *you*.

#2. *"We can't sign anyone who is not in the Screen Actors Guild."*

This is a useful one because it's both true *and* a lot of bullshit at the same time. It's true in terms of standard industry procedure, but there are all kinds of exceptions. More on that later. It's an easy out if it's late in the day and you're trying to clear the office. It's also popular because it can get rid of you for a nice long time. I fell for this one and believed it for nine years while concentrating on getting into the union. Of course, after finally getting my SAG card, I returned to many of the exact same agents proudly displaying it, only to find they just reverted to the next one on the list.

#3. *"We already have someone of your type."*

The first thing I thought was, you have a Dave Hern type? What type might that be? And even if there is someone that resembles me, you can only have one? What if he's busy working a job when a Dave Hern type role comes up? Of course, as you've probably deduced by now, what they are *really* saying is, "Please fuck off sir. And thank you very much." Nearly every rejection letter I've received from an agent concludes with the words "very truly yours." You know, I can't help but feel that anyone who was very truly mine wouldn't treat me that way.

#4. *"It's a slow period and we need to focus on the clients we already have."*

On one of the more memorable interviews, I met with an agent who was just a fount of stories of being besieged by the roster he already had. By the end of our meeting, he was pleading with me to sympathize with *his* workload. "I mean, Jesus, I can't even get work for the clients I've got, y'know? Please. *Please* try to understand!" I do. That doesn't help my situation. I know agents have a tough job. When you are a new agent, your job can be just as hard as acting, in terms of trying to get a foothold in the industry. They need successful clients in order to pay the bills and keep the doors open. The problem is, because of this, agents are not interested in your potential. They have a maddeningly short attention span. There are only so many hours in the day to make money and they are only interested in actors who are already bankable. You are a stranger to them. They don't want to say it out loud, but somehow, you must make the dollar signs go off in their eyes. Bottom line, they need to see something in you they think they can make money off.

One of the more exhausting truths is that by virtue of their position, they can also be as rude as they like toward you, while you are forced into tiptoeing delicately along the edges of people's egos. Yet, you've no doubt heard stories about some famous drunken actor breaking into strangers' houses and falling asleep, but his agent keeps giving him "one more chance" for another comeback? Apparently, once you get signed, you can then be as obnoxious and irresponsible as you like. How many other alcoholic burglars get that chance?

Of *course,* the Emmy winner thanks his agent and showers him with praise. They have a real relationship. They know each other and probably have a friendship in addition to their business relationship. That's the ideal kind of relationship for an actor to have with their agent. Unless of course, you don't have one. Then, you don't have _any_ kind of relationship.

One particular visit I recall as filled with irony. As I was sitting in a waiting area, an office employee wheeled a mail cart overflowing with actor's pictures and resumes right through the waiting area toward the trash. Then, a young actress breezed into the office and was welcomed inside by the agent. I then heard in detail the sound of an actress being signed. They exchanged information, collected pictures, welcomed their new client, and I could hear them chatting excitedly about their new possibilities. She thanked everyone and breezed back out. Then, it was my turn. Can you guess what they told me? They're not taking on any new clients right now. In this case, "right now" started in less than 30 seconds.

Of course, there is one other elephant in the room. It's called pretty. The blonde woman I saw that day was very pretty and pretty people tend to work in film and television because they look good on camera. Men or women. Agents snap them up all over. Of course, pretty people aren't pretty forever and the ones with acting chops have a better chance of surviving. Yes, folks, it's one of those unfair things in the world, but visually attractive people get all kinds of undue breaks in this life and that's nothing new.

Once, during the hunt, I stumbled into the boutique office of the personal manager to a major Hollywood star. He seemed amused at my tenacity and asked me some probing questions about what I was after, what my goals were, etc. He perfunctorily took my pix/res and sent me on the way with a handshake and a vaguely encouraging word. He was a Jewish guy from New York, just the kind of character I could easily see managing me. I regret to inform you that did not occur.

Just FYI, there is now a whole new layer to the process. I have heard that new actors today must have a prominent social media presence and a certain number of followers to even be considered by an agent. I'm so far behind that 8-ball, you can forget it. And looking for an agent has no statute of limitations, either. You can literally be looking for an agent until you die. I'm still holding out for the prize on that. So, don't waste your time, your postage, your printing costs, or your general happiness by cold calling and mailing stuff to people who don't know you. Save that energy for your next performance.

After a lot of these stupid battles, it became obvious a new plan was needed. Namely, to be seen acting. But how can you ever be seen acting if you're trapped in an office all day? This was a question I asked myself daily. A musician can throw open his guitar case and start playing on the street corner. Actors can't do that. Well, they can but it would look a little odd to see a bunch of guys doing Eugene O'Neil outside *Roscoe's Chicken and Waffles*. You need to perform in a venue you can invite people to. The continued pursuit of an agent led me down some pretty strange paths. For now, though, let's go back in time a bit . . .

16mm

The early 20th century is often regarded as a period of American history in black and white, largely due to newsreels and movies of the time. In my case, I remember it that way literally, because of my father's 16mm movie camera that he usually carried to the park to film his family. I loved looking through the lenses and putting the carrying case over my head. I would see the results later, on a large white screen beamed from his RCA 16mm projector, an amazing piece of expertly crafted steel machinery that made magic pictures.

Some of the earliest images I recall as a toddler are those of Charlie Chaplin and Buster Keaton ten feet tall on the screen of the *Bleecker Street Cinema*, the movie theater my father managed in Greenwich Village, New York City when I was born. It was there that I first became enamored by the alchemy of a moving visual image, its size and power over an audience. I would go up into the projection booth, behind the screen, and run up and down the aisles. This was when movies were transported in huge octagonal tin cans containing large metal reels. I was enthralled watching him thread the projectors with celluloid film, one of the first things I ever learned how to do. It was fascinating to learn the components of a movie image—sequential still pictures, seen through a rotating gate, projected on a screen, creating the illusion of motion. Amazing.

In his youth, my father Bernie Hern had been a vaudeville comic, touring with comedy/musical revues and doing stand-up comedy at clubs like the *Village Vanguard*. He appeared on the *Robert Q. Lewis Radio Show* in 1950 and the *Red Buttons Show* in 1954. He played gigs at "Adult Camps" which were entertainment resorts in the Catskills. His showbiz gigs were dispersed between many regular work jobs, from contracting and construction to standing on a factory line. He eluded the draft in WWII by being on tour with a Punch-and-Judy puppet troupe.

Returning to New York after touring in the road company of Ben Hecht's *The Front Page,* he was cast in his Broadway debut. As the show neared previews, one night his agent came backstage, took him aside, and quietly told him he had been replaced. Nothing much else needed to be said. It was 1954 and Senator Joseph McCarthy's senate subcommittee was in full swing branding people communists. My father was a *comedian*, not a communist. Maybe they couldn't spell it right. He was a comic who hung out a lot with other actors and writers, a klatch of coffee shop intellectuals who liked to throw jokes at each other, several of whom had liberal leanings. These people were a threat to no one. No person. No state. And even though he was never called before the committee, he was guilty by association. If you were even seen in the company of someone the Committee deemed suspect, you were part of a conspiracy. In my father's case, a conspiracy to come up with the best punchline.

He told me of an instance when as he was crossing the street in Manhattan and saw one of his oldest friends approaching, the friend spotted him in the crowd and immediately scooted to the other side of the street to avoid running into him. Because paranoia was de jour, there really was no fighting the reality that his comedy career was effectively over. It was shortly after this, he took the job at the movie theater for a few years until he was offered a position as an "art consultant" to a large savings and loan in California, which brought the family to the Golden State in the early 1960's.

Growing up, the lore of my father's showbiz career was something in the rearview mirror. I heard stories and the garage of our family home in Palo Alto contained a treasure trove of artifacts that kept me endlessly fascinated. One relic I loved perusing, and smelling, was my father's stage makeup kit from his theatre days—an authentic, multi-drawered professional kit which still contained old tubes of grease paint, powdered base, brushes, and spirit gum for hair appliances. With that and his dusty collapsible top hat, you were good to go. As a small child, one Halloween there was a community parade scheduled in downtown Palo Alto and using the kit, my father put the full Emmett Kelley clown face on me, which I displayed proudly for the crowd.

Other relics could be found in cardboard boxes full of reels of old 16mm film, some of which were real gems—genuine *Movie-Tone Newsreels* documenting everything from the doings of the 1950's congress to the winner of the Miss Miami one piece bathing suit competition. Those boxes always seemed to contain some new surprise like a few cartoons or commercials. I learned how to use a film editing bench and made a few stop-motion animated films with my state-of-the-art Super-8 camera.

Dad became the curator of a small museum in the lobby of a bank branch. The ever-changing exhibits featured relics of the US space program, famous puppets, toy trains, and every kind of art imaginable—sculptures, paintings, glassworks, and multi-media installations using light. He even built a miniature projection booth to show short films that informed the exhibits. And guess who had the job of manning it? Yes sir, and I even wrote out a showtime schedule. These influences were profound.

As a kid, it felt second nature to me to write skits and perform them. At five, I was put into the role of ringmaster of my kindergarten circus. I remember thinking it felt so natural to be hosting the show. The stage was such a comfortable place. If I'm ever asked, "When did you decide to be an actor?" I know it wasn't a decision. It was a *realization*—this is who I am and what I do. It was instinctive. There was no choice involved. If I was born in medieval times, my job would've been with the roving band of jesters and entertainers who traveled between townships, collecting the coins thrown at them before moving on.

MAGIC

Coming of age marinaded in art and all the trimmings, I dabbled in anything I could get my hands on. I learned how to play guitar. At the same time, I developed another major love— magic; practicing long and hard to develop a level of competence at basic sleight-of-hand (multiplying billiard balls, card tricks, stacking cups, etc.). I created my own schtick, a routine around the tricks, and amassed enough larger stage equipment over the years to work up an act which I advertised locally.

This turned out to be how I earned spending money all through school, doing my act at kids' birthday parties. It also gave me an early insight into audiences—the ways they behave and how to deal with them. I had a few great illusions in my set that I would build up to and save for the end. One involved displaying an empty tube that, after being sealed at both ends, produced an endless stream of colorful silks. Another produced a bowlful of popcorn that I would hand out to the kids to eat and keep them busy while I packed up. It was interesting to notice the difference in reactions between parents and children. For very young children, some of the best illusions weren't amazing to them at all because they accepted the premise that its *magic,* so they just enjoyed themselves anyway.

On the other end of the spectrum, some parents, embarrassed by the fact that they couldn't figure out how certain illusions were done would hover around me as I packed up to try and sneak a peek at the equipment. Some would ask directly, "Hey, how did you do that one with the tube? I mean, it's ok, you can tell me. I'm a grown-up." Others seemed annoyed at being fooled. Of course, I would always take the kids' position - it's *magic*. What I learned was that audiences, regardless of age, bring their lived experience into what they see when viewing art or a performance of any kind. Their beliefs, politics, and deepest feelings come into play whether it's a magic show, a movie, or a play. In that respect, the relationship between a performer and an audience is *always* very personal and people's reactions reveal more about themselves than anything else. So, treat your audiences as you would yourself. Without them, you're out of work.

Magic kept me in my own version of showbiz for most of my school years. By junior high school, I was writing and performing political stand-up routines in talent shows and appearing in either the school play or the local community production. This continued all through school and beyond. I also took to writing and recording radio parodies.

Right out of high school a significant event occurred. A local Bay Area-wide drama competition was announced. The first prize was a full scholarship to attend the American Conservatory Theatre's Actor's Training Program. I performed a scene from *Night Must Fall* by Emlyn Williams and won the competition. This was the biggest deal of my life up to that point, the first indication that I might be able to do this professionally. The following summer, I attended ACT's program and dove in headfirst. It was a deliciously thorough, intensive professional actor's education covering every aspect of theatre.

There were classes on everything from elocution and stage projection to Shakespearean period movement, taught by some of the best coaches I've ever had. While studying there, the great Vincent Price was staging a tour of his one-man show on the life of Oscar Wilde. My class was invited to watch him work a dress rehearsal where he was still calling for "line." It was fascinating and comforting to watch a legendary actor using the same tools all actors use to get to performance level. After all, this is the man who played "Dr. Goldfoot."

*NOTE: For those not familiar with the finer cinema of the 1960's, there was a series of American International Pictures entitled *Dr. Goldfoot and the Girl Bombs* and *Dr. Goldfoot and the Bikini Machine.* These brilliant films involved the evil Dr. Goldfoot, his sidekick Igor and their evil plot to take over the world with an army of bikini-clad exploding robots who seduce heads of state by kissing them and blowing them up. Now *that's* showbiz, kids. The plots were so juvenile and the dialogue so moronic, I always wondered how such a dignified man could bring himself to be seen in such stupid drivel.

Over his rehearsal cycle, he stepped into a class or two to guest coach, which was a thrill because not only did I have a chance to be directed by him, but there was also a burning question that needed to be asked. How did he like doing the *Dr. Goldfoot* movies? I will never forget his response. He threw his head back, bunched up his fists and laughed, bobbing up and down, embracing himself. "Oh, I *LOVED* it! I absolutely *LOVED* it!! It was *Won*-der-full!" This really registered with me. You have to love it. In the long run, nothing else really matters. When you love it, any opportunity to do it is a blessing. Even if it's the dumbest thing on earth. There are worse ways to earn a living. If there's a <u>Lesson Number One</u>, this is it. If you're not having big fat fun, what on earth are you doing there? That's an indicator maybe you should be somewhere else. For me, it's always been the actual *doing* of it. That's the reward. I'm getting dessert upfront. Just doing it is more fun than anything that may come as a result, *including* money.

ACT's founder and artistic director, William Ball was a gifted man I will remember for his ebullient love of theatre. His childlike excitement was infectious and permeated the place, in the hubbub of activity, in the halls and classrooms, in the feel of possibility. It was such a welcoming place, devoted entirely to the development of new theatrical ideas. It inspired me to shoot a mini documentary of my experience there which was screened for the full academy at our closing session. I came away from that experience exhilarated and well trained in theatre, but not ready at all for what I would face after I packed up my life and moved to Hollywood.

MARCHING IN

In the late 1960's, early 70's, Louis B. Mayer, Samuel Goldwyn, and the other big studio bosses began to pass away, creating a short-lived vacuum in studio management. This spawned a brief period of the "auteur" filmmaker, when writers, directors, and a new generation of "off-beat" actors jumped into the creative breach and took control. This was the time of groups like Coppola's *American Zoetrope*. I felt a real kinship with this crowd and envisioned a similar path. But growing up on the films of the 70's gave me a false understanding of the possibilities of American cinema. It was such a free-wheeling, artistically open space and the turmoil of the times fueled challenging stories, full of ambiguity and irony which to me is the most exciting kind of art. I didn't understand this was an anomaly, a fleeting period of unsupervised creativity that wouldn't last. By the 80's when I arrived, the major studios already had their arms back around the cash machine and had verticalized with near total corporate ownership producing tentpole franchises with massive marketing campaigns.

So, here I come marching into town, thinking that I'm going to be able to walk through it all, continuing the radical tradition of art. So, what do you do first? On my second night in town, I found myself in a cabin behind the house of a famous Hollywood director from the 70's that I greatly admired. His son and a small group of friends lived in this cabin out back and were sitting around quipping about the industry and strangely sniping at each other. They spent the whole evening making nasty, sarcastic comments about celebrities and people in the business. Every time I asked a question, they looked at each other with a knowing little snicker and said nothing. Guess I was the new fish. It was weird to be both welcomed and excluded at the same time. Is this the way the son of a famous director acts? I made no effort to schmooze the guy and didn't see much reason for hanging around. OK, I thought, well that wasn't pleasant. Hope it gets better.

The world of theatre, of rehearsal and live performance, had been my home for so long that when I moved to LA, I had every intention of continuing theatre as a way of parlaying it into a film career. I didn't expect getting on stage to be as difficult as everything else there. I auditioned for plays, but most of the town is busy trying to get into movies and TV, so showcasing tends to be de jour. Showcases are evenings of scenes presented for industry professionals. The movie biz is driven by different motives than regional theatre companies.

I began to spend a lot of time at *Nosotros*, a Latino theatre organization and playhouse founded by actor Ricardo Montalban. They held showcases, staged original performances, and held various classes. My friends and associates were there, so I kind of fell in with the group, found a good coach there, joined his class and put in some hard scene work with an eye on showcasing. Over time, I got to know almost the entire Latino acting population of Hollywood. Of course, Hollywood as a purveyor of stereotypes creates a landscape where a lot of Hispanic actors are still cast as gardeners, waiters, maids, bus drivers, etc., with only a select few in prominent roles.

Ricardo Montalban was keenly aware of this which led to the founding of the group in the first place—to broaden the profile of Latino talent in the industry and to fuel theatrical productions featuring Hispanic performers in leading roles.

Being back around a hub of creative activity felt great. Now, how do we snap us up an agent? I found a scene from the play *Thieves* by Herb Gardner, a beautiful little vignette involving Martin and Sally, a couple who are continually breaking up. They get together to discuss a divorce and end up sharing a bottle of wine and sleeping together again which of course stirs up all kinds of confusing emotions. A great little set piece. I asked Flo, an actress friend, to be my Sally. I would have liked her to be more, but that's another story. Flo was involved with a guy I thought was way too boring for her and I teased her about it a lot. This made for a pretty rich environment that both paralleled and fueled the energy of the scene. We worked well together. Our rhythm and energy onstage felt natural and funny, so we put in a good bit of rehearsal time with an eye on the upcoming fall showcase the playhouse was staging. Of course, being that the scene involved laying around half naked in bed with Flo, it was a test of my professionalism.

I felt great about the scene and knew that if the audience was comprised of the right industry people, we had a good shot at either an agent, a casting director, or manager. Flo was in search of management too and was hopeful.

The showcase was well promoted and the audience filled the house on show night. Ricardo Montalban showed up as well, which put an extra measure of pressure on all of us to deliver for the man himself. Our scene came near the end, so for most of the show, Flo and I warmed up backstage listening to all the scenes. When we heard our intro music and the scene-change lights went down, we walked on stage and got into our bed. From the moment the stage lights came up, every moment felt like the first time and the audience response was so strong, I was a little shocked. We landed every laugh line, which is always the best instant reward, and the more emotional moments felt just right. The scene ends with Sally walking out, leaving Martin with his head in his hands. As the lights faded, the applause was so loud that I ran backstage and punched the sky a few times. It felt like we hit a bullseye. A rare moment of knowing that we delivered.

The first person to come backstage was Ricardo Montalban who approached and grabbed my hand. "Excellent work," he said. "Excellent work." I kept saying, "thank you" mostly because I couldn't think of anything else. I ducked into the dressing room to put clothes on and get out of makeup quickly so I could do some mingling. Flo was busy with that when I came out, but after 10, 20, then 30 minutes of chatting and watching people thank each other and head out the door, I started feeling strange. Wait, I thought, where are all the agents with pre-written contracts in hand, swarming to get to me first? This was a moment of profound learning. I was genuinely bewildered and confused. Everything I had done since arriving in LA had led up to this moment and we knocked it out of the park. I remember thinking, well that's some of the best I have in me to sell, so if that doesn't do it, I might be in trouble. I also might have paid more attention to that thought.

UNIONS

The other major requirement for any kind of career is membership in the Screen Actors Guild. There used to be a separate union called the American Federation of Television and Radio Artists. The two unions merged in 2012 to form SAG-AFTRA which is now the only major actor's union for the entire film industry. You must be a member of the union in order to work.

How do you get in the union? Take a guess. You can't. You only get in the union if you've already worked professionally. Got it? You're not allowed to work without a union card, and you can't get a union card unless you've worked. Translation—*you can't get in the union, pal.* Unless you're *lucky.* Let's just say that out loud, ok? **LU-*CKY*.** Unless there's a freak accident.

Think of it. There is a huge union office building in Los Angeles with rooms and rooms of desks, copiers, supplies, telephones, computers, and a full staff of employees who work all day calculating and securing the earnings and benefits of the <u>fortunate</u>. Less than 5% of the entire membership of the Screen Actors Guild is actually working at any given time. How many people do you think would go to medical school if they were told in advance there's only a 5% chance you'll ever practice medicine?

Here's how it happened for me. I auditioned for an ultra-low budget non-union movie. Upon meeting the director, we hit it off well and after my reading, he hired me on the spot. The scene involving my character was scheduled to shoot within a couple of days. It was a great little part that required some hard work. I did the job and had a great time. Shortly afterwards, the movie company signed an agreement with SAG to go union. Since my scene was already in the can before the company went signatory with SAG, the union had to admit me after the fact through a "Taft-Hartley" agreement. Had it not been for this happenstance of events, I might easily have never been admitted to the guild.

It's hard to forget what a grueling, next to impossible enterprise getting a union card was. And yet, at the same time, if you are already wanted for an important role, it can all be bypassed and contractually corrected in a heartbeat. Think about child actors. Were they born in the Screen Actors Guild? No, but they need child actors to play children, so those details get taken care of. People who are grandfathered into the industry early tend to forget how murderously difficult it is to get over those hurdles. As a result, I came to believe that a SAG card was Wonka's golden ticket, a magic door pass to the land of Oz. Then, after finally getting a union card, I quickly found out that it changed absolutely nothing. As mentioned, the very same agents who showed me the front door without a union card showed me the back door *with* one. In fact, you now have the privilege of remaining unemployed in a *narrower* pool of jobs. There is always more non-union than union work out there. Once you join, you are no longer permitted to do any non-union work.

You're in a brand-new limbo. Actors without agents have one of two choices—remain non-union, get some gigs, but without a real shot at major professional level work, OR join the union, get a new bill in the mail, another card in your wallet and go back to your day job.

If it were up to me, there would be only one criterion for a SAG card. Can you act and do it well? Show us. You can? Fine, here's your SAG card. If you can't, sorry, no license to act. Just like the DMV or the Bar Exam—something you have to pass to be considered legitimate and that you can take as many times as you need to pass. This would have the added benefit of keeping really bad actors off the screen. They must improve before they can get into the guild.

Here's some more odd things. Membership in most unions comes with a suite of benefits immediately upon joining— medical, dental, family coverage, wage tables, 401(k), pension plan. Not so in showbiz. The benefits you receive from SAG are ONLY if you've worked and earned *enough* to reach a qualifying threshold. If not, you receive no benefits at all. Possibly ever. As of this writing, your humble servant has been a proud SAG member for 37 years and still does not qualify for a dime of union benefits. And yet, I have always paid my dues on time. It feels a little like a one-sided relationship. Just as with an agent, a percentage of your earnings will go to the union. They calculate your annual dues based on your income. You are asked to complete an income statement every year and pay dues whether you're working or not. The more you work, the more dues you pay. Also, you must work for a full decade to become vested for a pension.

So, what DO you get for your dues money? Well, the one thing *every* member does get is a subscription to SAG-AFTRA magazine. Each issue has different pictures of celebrities smiling in group shots at awards ceremonies and mingling at union events. There are lengthy articles about the latest contract negotiations and events for different causes, like the Actor's Retirement Home. I knew many actors who dove into its pages religiously every month and would discuss it at length. I must confess that personally, I always found it rather annoying—a unique form of torture; a glossy color window into a world of benefits you may never receive and parties you will never attend; a monthly reminder of the career that you don't actually have. The union also asks you to vote on various contracts and leadership nominees. There's an expectation of you to maintain a trooper attitude and be actively involved in union affairs even if nothing you vote on ever has any direct effect on your life or career. You're supposed to go directly from being perpetually stonewalled to immediate fealty. Be a loyal team member even if the coach *never* lets you play. Do it for your fellow actors. We're all in this together, right? You can also open a free credit union account.

Allow me a moment's clarification here to leave no doubt that politically, I am absolutely a union man all the way. Always have been. I whole-heartedly support the right to strike, collective bargaining rights, and for actors who are lucky enough to work, the union is exceptional in the way it oversees employees' wages and working conditions. And I am extremely grateful there is a well-functioning union since for years actors had no say or leverage in decisions affecting their work lives. But, if you don't work because you don't have an agent, they don't do a thing for you.

Sorry to keep mentioning that, but it keeps sitting there like an elephant. So, I'll leave it like this. I support my union in the same way they support me—on a contingency basis. Another tool you get access to is the *Residuals Calculator* on the union website. For working people, this development is extremely helpful since today there are so many formats and platforms for actors' work to be sold to. In the past, this made tracking one's income very difficult. The calculator is a simplified breakdown of your residual earnings in an easy format for you to use as a planner and for tax info. Every once in a while, since I'm eligible and for a little amusement, I log on, enter my very own calculator, and just for fun I make up a dialogue of me on the phone with my accountant.

> "Hey Bill, got all the data broken down for ya. Ok?"
> "Great, Dave. So, adjusted gross income?"
> "Zero."
> "Earned income credit?"
> "Zero. What'd you say? Interest income? Oh, let me check. Uh . . . that would be zero."
> "How about qualified business income?"
> "Yep, looks like zero."
> "Is that zero *point* zero or . . .?"
> "No that's zero point zero zero, with five zeroes after that."

"Great. Thanks. Should be a banner tax year."

"Love ya, babe. Gotta go open that free credit union account."

Now, if the oceans of the world part and you do have a "qualifying event" (*accident*) and after you've paid your initiation fee and current dues, the guild finally runs out of reasons to exclude you. So, they will schedule an "intake session" which used to be held in the SAG offices. I remember walking into that building feeling so proud, but pretty exhausted too. I had a head full of questions about the entire deal. I also felt a weird sense of survivor's guilt. What about all the others who ten minutes ago I was in the same boat with? I'm special now because I tripped over something?

We were placed into a room that looked like a college lecture hall. After we all sat down, two tall young blonde men bounced into the room wearing tennis shoes and pullover sweaters with the SAG logo on them. They waved their hands like hosts of a Saturday morning kid's TV show. "Hey everybody, my name's Bobby and this is Hank. We're here to say congrats, give you guys a big welcome, and to answer all your questions about the guild, benefits, and anything else that might be on your mind." They then gave us a pretty thorough overview of all the benefits that we theoretically *may* be eligible for somewhere over the rainbow. When Bobby and Hank were finished, they threw it open to the group and my hand shot up immediately.

"Yes, why is it so impossible to get here? Why did it take nine years to . . ." Bobby jumped in, cleared his throat, and raised his voice, talking over me. "Well, um . . . _how_ you get here is _your_ business. We're just here to let you know what to expect from the guild and what the rules and regulations are."

I had asked the forbidden question. The one nobody really knows the answer to. This was another lesson. A lot of the industry is predicated on illusion so it's best to accept that a lot of it makes no sense and not to expect it to. Certainly not out loud. You have to adjust to it. Sometimes opposing things can be true at the same time. The union has bunches of rules and bylaws that must be followed whether you personally think they're logical, fair, etc. It's just part of the deal.

For example, let's say you are a SAG actor who lives in Albuquerque, and you have a shot at a part in a movie in Los Angeles. Sounds great. Time to book a flight, right? Not so fast. If the movie is non-union, you can't do the job at all. Remember? SAG Rule # 1 is no more non-union work or you can be penalized or suspended from the guild. If the movie _is_ union and you don't live in Los Angeles, under SAG rules, the production <u>must</u> pay for your travel, accommodations, and a per diem. Most low budget movie companies don't want to have to pay that, so instead they hire local actors to avoid those costs. So, you say, "What if I cover my own expenses? The production won't have to pay." Sorry. Against the rules. You're not allowed to do that either. If they want to save money, they will offer it to a local actor.

Look, I get it. These rules are secured for the workers. That's what a union is for. And it's not an issue for huge media companies or A-list actors who are used to these arrangements, but for many others they represent additional disqualifiers. Effectively, they've made it so that everyone in showbiz must live in LA to have a workable career. But wait, you may ask, didn't Robin Williams live in San Francisco and Woody Allen in New York? Yes. That's because they're stars, and well-established actors can live wherever the fuck they want to. Are you getting all this down? For every rule, there's a situation that trumps it.

So, let's recap where we are so far. You can't get an agent and you can't get a union card and there's no point in mailing things to strangers and you shouldn't be talking about, much less writing about any of this. So, what the hell are you left with? Isn't there a short cut? OK, if you insist . . .

Quick list of things you can do to make it big in showbiz:

1.   Make sure to be born very physically attractive.

2.   Marry into a well-established showbiz family.

3.   Become *extraordinarily* fortunate.

4.   Live next door to a studio head.

5.   Date the son / daughter of a studio head.

6.   Believe in your dreams.

JOBS

I've always considered jobs to be a colossal intrusion and interference with my creative life. And it's certainly not like I didn't see it coming. I recall as a five or six-year-old kid, knowing and feeling in my gut that the employment train was coming right at me and that I could only avoid it for so long. I thought, "You mean, I'm going to have to spend all day, every day of my life doing stuff I don't care about, just so I can eat and sleep and come back and do it again? What a nightmare!" I knew inside, even at that age that the things I was born to do were somehow not going to be compatible with earning a reliable living and it scared me even then as I saw it approaching. Then, the train hit me, knocked me down and rolled right over me for the next 38 years.

Yolanda sat in front of me in tears. She was the matriarch of a large Filipino family, an employee everybody liked at one of the onsite law-firm copy centers I managed. I had just delivered her performance review in which I had given her exceptional marks. I had also given her a 4% raise— the maximum allowed by the company. I had listed "reducing phone time" as a "goal"—without it having any effect on her raise or job level. This was during the time before iPhones, when there was only one extension to call for the copy center. Her family was so huge that the main business line had been ringing all day, requiring her to stop work, walk over to the main counter where the phone was, take her call, then walk back to her machine and resume her copy job. I had begun to get complaints from customers that they were unable to reach the copy center by phone and the workflow was slowing so they weren't getting their documents on time. I told her about this, without putting it in her review. But the damage was done. She told me I didn't care about single mothers and I couldn't possibly understand. She said I had no sympathy for people in her situation. I was giving her a lousy raise to punish her. All I cared about was my position. I had ruined her day. Inside, I knew the company was all I represented to her. How could she know anything else? Oh, how I wished to tell her of the agonies and ironies roiling inside me. In a parallel world, I would have spilled it all.

"Yolanda, I'm an actor. If you only knew how much I don't give a shit about this, about even being here, going through this with you. I don't care about the company. If I was in your position, I wouldn't trust me either. Another white guy with a tie making decisions on your life. I don't want this position. I hate giving you this review as much as you hate getting it. I wish I could get my old film editor and splice both of us out of this movie and into another one where we run into each other on a boardwalk somewhere and share ice cream cones with you and your whole family. That's what I would like. I wish I could just make a break for it and run away from this entire tragic ritual. I'm another working guy who got stuck in this corporate dance with you. I'm sorry."

This memory saddens me particularly because in the modern world, Yolanda could have talked to her family on a Bluetooth earpiece *while* she did her work without interrupting anything or bothering anybody. Instead, in the pre-techno world, I had to ruin her life. I hope God doesn't hold that against me on judgement day, which I hope isn't anything like a performance review.

When I first got thrown out into the work world, all I knew how to do was thread projectors with 16mm film. Not a skill in demand. Also, I didn't have much brawn for blue collar work, so I took more white-collar type jobs than I can even remember. I worked every shift known to man. I was a bank teller, copy machine operator, legal file clerk, mail clerk, substitute teacher, corporate trainer, computer tape librarian, receptionist, customer account manager, part-time employee, and full-time miserable guy. I have always admired any artist who actually manages to survive off their craft. And I mean *any* artist. Any painter, sculptor, musician, filmmaker, jeweler, dancer, mime, clown, glass blower, sidewalk chalk man, whatever. Unfortunately, we do not live in a society that provides much support for the artist, so if you have the ingenuity to make it pay, you win in my book.

There are two kinds of actors. Those that earn a living at it and those that do not. The vast majority of all actors since the beginning of time are in the second category. The real number of actors who actually earn a living at it is infinitesimal. Many European countries regard the performing arts as a legitimate craft and it's common to find stage actors frequently on the public "dole" to bridge an employment gap. In America, it's sink or swim. You make money at it, or you do not. Unemployment runs out. By American consumer standards, you aren't even considered a real actor unless you are earning a living at it, which is just incorrect. There are plenty of performers in community theatre, non-union films, and other venues who most certainly are actors. They're just actors with other jobs as well. If you hear a woman playing the violin and she's extremely good, if she then serves your pizza, does that mean she isn't really a musician? Leave a good tip, by the way.

I never fully found an employable task or function to sustain myself that didn't also depress the hell out of me and drive me nuts. I can never shut off the screenplay that's always writing itself in my head. Or the character I'm developing, weaving through my consciousness. It's a form of madness, really—an affliction. Even so, I must have been relatively competent at my jobs since I kept getting promoted in spite of myself. At several of the facilities management companies I worked for, I went from copy operator to middle management to upper middle management within a few years. I still believe it's because I looked the part. I'm a tall, thin white guy who could wear a suit, smile, shake hands, and talk the talking points, etc.

So, I spent a large part of my life stuck in this strange duality where every day, people in show business are telling me to get lost. Yet, also every day, as I play the part of an account manager, my co-workers are saying, "What are you doing here, Dave? You should be in show business!" When you're really an actor but have to survive in the work world, life becomes a shadow existence. And in LA, you come out of the gate with a few deficits because in the regular work world, people frown on actors as potential hires because they have a reputation for being flaky, unreliable, and problematic. And with good cause too, so most actors keep it a secret from their employers.

Here's an example of why. Once, I was a bank teller with no agent, so through a casting assistant I had met, lo and behold, I procured an audition for Steven Bochco's *Hill Street Blues*, one of the top TV shows of the time. I had a rigid work schedule but there was no way I could miss this chance. The bank branch where I worked was in Century City and the casting office was in the San Fernando Valley. I had a tight one-hour lunch break, so in my mind, I had planned the whole thing out like a tactical military operation. I brought a bag lunch in tow and kept a close eye on my watch all morning. I was so nervous, I had trouble concentrating on work.

As lunch hour approached, I walked casually out the front door, then made a breaking run for the parking garage. I jumped into the backseat of my car where I had planted a change of clothes, wriggled out of my business suit, and put on the T-shirt and jeans that more fit the character. I then proceeded to break a bunch of speed limits while stuffing my face with a tuna sandwich and messing up my hair to look scruffier. Luckily, the traffic was sparse, and I actually managed to maneuver fast enough to arrive at the casting office in Studio City within five minutes of audition time. Purely by the grace of God, they were on schedule, and I was called in almost immediately.

It was a final round since Steven Bochco was present along with two writers and the casting director. Now, I am not sure if it was all the nervous energy or the frantic circumstances, but I absolutely killed it. It was maybe the best audition I have ever done. I felt happy, relaxed, and completely comfortable with the dialogue. I even got a laugh out of Bochco. They were so responsive and upbeat, I thought I had a serious shot. I literally went dancing out of the casting office, with a little shuffle and a ballet leap out the door. Then, it was immediately back in the car, navigating Mulholland Drive like a maniac, keeping an eye out for cops while finishing an apple. I pulled in the bank's underground parking lot, leaped into the back seat where I changed back into my suit and made for the elevators. Were it not for a broken floor button, I would have only been 5 instead of 10 minutes late. "Did you have a nice lunch?" one of my co-workers asked. "Fine," I said. "Great... thanks." And for the record, I balanced out to the penny that night.

I once saw a revealing interview with Jack Lemmon about his career. He openly admitted that chance and blind luck saved his life. He made a ducking gesture and wiped his brow. "Whew!" he said. "I sure am lucky I had success as an actor because I was never very good at anything else. I don't think I could have held a regular work job." When I heard this, I said out loud, "Yeah, you and me Jack! Only you had the career."

If you're like me, you like to eat and unless you want to do crime, you may need a job. So, I did lots of them, but looking back, I'm damned if I can find much significance in any of them. One day, working as a copy machine operator, I had to work a double shift. The first ended at midnight and the second began at 7:00 am. So, I decided to stay all night. Attorneys had a document production for an industrial accident case due the next day.

On my feet pumping copies into the night, I couldn't help but notice these were not just *any* copies. In addition to the case documents and receipts, there were large color photographs of the accident scene itself. A construction worker on the ground was helping guide a crane operator to place a section of wall down over vertically cemented rebar. The crane collapsed on top of the worker impaling him face down on the rebar which stuck right through his head and neck. It was the most ghastly, horrid set of pictures I've ever seen. And not only was I forced to look at these horrific, gruesome images, shot from every grotesque angle, I needed to do quality control which required examining them up close. To this day, those images are burned into my brain. They made me feel mighty fragile. I thought, "Lord, save me from a death like that or from having to witness one."

Later, with my jacket rolled up and tucked under my head for a pillow, I spent the night curled up in the corner of a conference room floor in one of the tallest high-rise office buildings in downtown Los Angeles. Laying there in the dark, staring at the ceiling, I found myself thinking about that construction worker, just another guy on the job, like any other day. Please don't let me die on the job. I subjected myself to all of this for a few overtime hours.

I didn't have a family to support, so all I was living for was my dream of deliverance. I had a recurring vision. My lunch breaks were usually in any number of skyscrapers facing different directions. So, in the lunchrooms, I would always scout for a window seat to look out over the horizon. I saw myself in slow-motion, diving through the plate glass windows, and soaring out over sunlit hills and colorful valleys on massive, glistening butterfly wings. I could fill my lungs with fresh air and see for miles in every direction. My flights filled me with a vital, bracing sense of the beauty of nature and the preciousness of life. Until of course, I had to go back to the file room.

At one point in my interminable office life, fortune did raise a hand slightly when I was moved into the position of corporate trainer which the company realized would be a better use of my skill set. I now had business cards with the company logo on them. You know how corporations periodically come up with new insignias and lingos? I became responsible for all new hire orientations and various other "roll-outs" of company "initiatives" that needed "implementation." All this means is, I got to stand up in front of people and give them the spiel. I would watch in amazement as my co-workers quickly adopted whatever terms and buzz words were necessary to function.

I did have a script to follow—a pre-created curriculum entitled *Quality People Providing Quality Service*, a program created by a training think tank with eight "modules" covering rules, policies, forms, and procedures that all employees needed to know. I tried my best to at least make it entertaining. Luckily, management gave me a measure of room to spice it up a bit so I threw in some *Far Side* cartoons on overheads, put a few jokes on the big easel pads, and came up with enough banter to fill each session. They even gave me a collapsible pointer which helped me look like a professor or at least someone who knows something.

There was also a company produced video I needed to incorporate. More moments of irony here because guess who was in the videos? Yup. Actors. Who I'm sure were also happy to have a job. In fact, I had done a few industrial films that were exactly like them. This particular one instructed people how not to be an intolerable asshole on the job and how to actually help people instead of getting in their way. Well, I sure did get to know those actors well because by the end of that summer, I had sat through the video probably 50 times. I was a captive audience along with my trainees.

All in all, though, it was a more tolerable period of work which made for more quality time spent *elsewhere*—in rehearsal and on all my other plots and schemes.

CASTING

How do actors get parts in movies and TV? Ok, basically it goes like this. Let's say a producer of a movie or TV show has a script that is green-lighted for production, meaning someone is bankrolling it. The screenplay will then be "broken down" into a list of character descriptions known as "The Breakdowns." The service that performs this function is called *Breakdown Services Ltd.* The resulting list of character descriptions is a proprietary document that *only* franchised agents receive. Why? No time for that now. Breakdowns look like this:

ANDREW TOLLIVER – 40's, white, medium build, prematurely grey. The owner of a small, high-end cruise line. With his marriage falling apart, he is personally frustrated in spite of his success. He secretly wishes he could sell everything and go live on the Irish countryside.

NEWTON BERRY – 50's, tall, African American. A sharply dressed, smooth-talking lawyer who represents Andrew in a divorce. He can be ruthless in court. He understands the game and how to play it. At home though, he is very much the loving family man.

Now, every TV or movie production hires a casting director. And as previously discussed, most actors are represented by agents. After reading the breakdowns, agents submit pix/res of their clients to the casting directors of the studio or production. It is then the casting director's job to sort through all the incoming pix/res and select a small handful of actors per role to audition. Again, this was all done by snail mail in the pre-digital age. The casting director is the narrow-downer. This process applies to casting most roles *except* for the stars who usually are selected by the director and/or producers and their contracts are negotiated independently with their agents.

Here's another area where actors make jerks out of themselves by trying to kiss up to casting people. What they forget is, no matter how much they may like you personally or how great an actor they may think you are, they can't *make* a role that fits you. For example, if the breakdown describes a 300 lb. Asian sumo wrestler and you are a tall, skinny Irish guy, you will not be called for that part. And if, by some mistake, you *were* called, that production would probably fire their casting director. It's important to understand that they have to make sure the actors they audition at least resemble the roles they're casting. There's a difference between being versatile and being unrealistic. If you are a five-foot two chubby white woman, you cannot very well play the role of a muscular, six-foot nine, African American basketball player. There is no such thing as "fairness" in casting and that's not a gripe, it's a helpful fact. If you don't get a role because you don't look like the character, does that mean the decision is unfair? No. It could very well be the right decision for the character regardless of whether you happen to fit the part or not.

Understanding this takes a lot of heat off yourself. There are so many reasons why you will or will not be cast in a given role. That's why I've never been particularly concerned about the reasons for not getting a part. Some actors think if they hear all the specific reasons, they can then make some "adjustments" to be better and get the part next time. But of course, next time is an entirely different confluence of script, people, and circumstances that there really is no way to prepare for. Don't waste your mental energy anticipating. Relax and be open to whatever might come along.

The week following my manic audition for *Hill Street Blues*, I found out I did not get the part. I was certainly disappointed to not be working, but I suspected it was a casting decision unrelated to what I delivered at the audition. I had no doubt I had given one hundred and two percent that day. When the episode aired, I saw that the actor they had chosen was an orthodox Jewish man, twice my age and three times my weight. It was obvious what their character choice was and why. This was one of my first lessons about the audition / casting process. There are always factors at work that you may not be privy to. All you can do is deliver your very best and leave it be. There is really no magic audition formula. Each one is an individual challenge.

Now, there's an exception to the casting process I've outlined here. An established actor's stature can sometimes change the way casting decisions are made. For example, take Jack Nicholson's performance as Randall Patrick McMurphy in the classic movie *One Flew Over the Cuckoo's Nest*. For readers of Ken Kesey's book, McMurphy is described as a tall, barrel-chested man who whoops and hollers like a cowboy, sports tufts of red hair, garish red sideburns, and a prominent wine-colored scar on his nose. He has tattoos on his shoulders and on the knuckles of his massive, calloused hands. Nicholson clearly wasn't that. But his ability to get McMurphy's contentious, anti-establishment persona won out. Plus, obviously his star power didn't hurt. Once again, stars bend the rules.

But, not so for us slobs. In fact, if you don't follow the rules, they may hunt you down. I once came across some contraband copies of the week's breakdowns. I don't remember how they came into my possession, probably from another actor. So, I used them to make submission suggestions to an agent. Well, little did I know that soon, while faxing my life away at work, I would receive a phone call from what I can only call "The Breakdown Police." A stern voice reprimanded me for having the document and trying to use it to help my career. The first thing I wondered was how on earth they got my work phone number. You mean, this is important enough to research? Ok, I broke the rules. I have hostages. You'll never take me alive. I fessed up just to finish the call, but I did ask him, "You've never heard of this before? I can't be the first actor in history to have got ahold of some breakdowns." I never heard from the breakdown police again, so I'm assuming they dismissed the charges.

Yes, how dare I try to pull myself out of the swamp? How dare I try to attempt a life of art and creativity? Who the hell do I think I am? An actor?

SUPERHUMAN

On the night of June 16, 1959, actor George Reeves held a small get together in his home in Benedict Canyon. As the evening wore on and everyone was properly drunk, he wished his guests a goodnight, trudged up the stairs, and blew his brains out with a small caliber pistol. He was 45 years old. Reeves was famous for playing the original *Superman* in the TV serial, so naturally the headlines the next day were full of references to the "man of steel" who "couldn't stop a speeding bullet."

There were a few conflicting stories regarding his death. Reeves had been having an affair with a woman named Toni Mannix who was the ex-showgirl wife of MGM vice president, Eddie Mannix, a known "fixer" with suspected mob ties. Also, Reeves' then fiancé Leonore Lemmon, a society girl who was present at the party, was questioned by police during the investigation. A few of these scenarios were explored in the 2006 movie *Hollywoodland* with Ben Affleck. Despite those suspicions and some inconsistencies, ultimately Reeves' autopsy report and the physical evidence led to his death being officially ruled a suicide. And so it remains.

But the aspect of George Reeves' story that always jumped out at me was not his tabloid death, but rather his view of his own life. His story reveals a lot about showbiz that is worth noticing. In 1939, he was cast in *Gone with the Wind* as Stuart Tarleton, one of Scarlett O'Hara's suitors in the film's opening scene. Pretty amazing luck. Right out of the gate, plopped straight into the hugest studio movie of its time. Imagine what that can do to a young actor's fragile ego? This was when actors were contracted to film studios for multiple picture deals, so he signed with Warner Brothers, where he appeared in two films with Ronald Reagan and three with James Cagney, none of which garnered him any real attention. His contract with Warner Brothers ended up being dissolved by mutual consent.

He then signed with 20th Century Fox, but after co-starring opposite Merle Oberon in the 1941 film *Lydia*, which was a box office failure, Fox released him after only a few pictures. He was then forced to freelance for a while. He screen-tested for his appearance in five of the *Hop-Along Cassidy* westerns. This led to a significant role opposite Claudette Colbert in the war drama, *So Proudly We Hail!* which resulted in Paramount signing him for two films a year. But making that film inspired him so much, he instead decided to put his entire career on hold to enlist in the U.S. Army. Take note. He made a decision to walk away. After the war, a lot of film production in Hollywood had dried up or stopped altogether. He was reduced to acting in cheap serials and took a side job digging cesspools.

In 1951, Reeves was offered the role of *Superman* in a new television series. Many actors who saw themselves as movie stars viewed television as beneath them. It meant taking a step down in one's career, not something to be taken seriously. Reeves was very reluctant but took the job that paid $5,000 a week—easily ten times that amount in today's equivalent dollars.

The pilot movie and first season were shot back-to-back and were purchased by what was then a struggling ABC network to be broadcast nationally, which instantly made him a worldwide celebrity, something he never expected and never fully adjusted to.

He was suddenly besieged by adoring throngs of children wanting autographs and answers to all their questions. He earned extra money from making personal appearances, where he took his status as a role-model seriously enough to always be fatherly, supportive, and to never be seen smoking cigarettes. But privately, he confessed to a certain level of embarrassment. After a while, it became more of a duty than a joy. He once referred to "this monkey suit" and more than once was heard saying, "Here I am, wasting my life." He made a few attempts to launch movie projects of his own; a few got to the development stage, but none ever got off the ground.

So, what can we conclude about this man's mindset? And why am I referencing his story? Well, in addition to being one of those kids who really enjoyed *The Adventures of Superman*, now as an adult actor, it makes me sad to realize that I probably had more fun and got more joy out of watching him work then he did actually doing it. What we see is a man perpetually dissatisfied with his stature in the industry, always looking over his shoulder at the careers of others. He wanted to be Clark Gable, the leading man. He forgot <u>Lesson Number One.</u> He forgot to enjoy his life. And he completely missed his own career, *while it was happening.* Instead, he spent it feeling restless and slighted, like he never got his due. In that respect, he's a tragic figure. Ben Affleck captured this perfectly in his performance, showing us a man with a massive chip on his shoulder, the polar opposite of his contemporary, Vincent Price.

It's ironic that George Reeves is now revered as an indelible figure in the pantheon of classic television pioneers. He may not have been the best actor, but he will forever be the original, and I would argue the best Superman. And when you look at his list of lifetime credits, it's impressive. Two best pictures—*Gone with the Wind, From Here to Eternity*—a dozen more feature films and more than a dozen live television plays on programs such as *Kraft Television Theatre* which are now considered classics as well. And in a final irony, Reeves had often said he might have felt better about his most famous role if he knew there were any grownups out there watching. What he never learned was that *The Adventures of Superman* had a huge adult audience even during its original run. Never mind the millions of video copies that have been purchased by adults to this day.

As a child, I had no idea he had already passed and didn't learn of his suicide until my teens. So, his story is for me a cautionary tale. One about gratitude for what you have. A reminder of the impermanence of life and most certainly of a career in Hollywood. Neither one comes with any guarantees, so if you don't enjoy it while it's actually taking place, you're missing the whole point. You can't rewind the movie. There's only one showtime.

A quick note on...CARS

I don't care about them. Not at all. I went through four of them in ten years—a grey Plymouth Valiant, a silver Honda Accord, a red Chevy Camaro, and a green Pontiac Heap of Shit. To some guys, they're a reflection of basic masculinity, a symbol of manhood on display. I consider them four wheels that get me to a destination, preferably in one piece. When you don't have money, daily existence becomes a cycle of relentless auto maintenance, a steel parking boot on your life.

Over time, the Plymouth had small pieces broken off or taken—the antenna, the battery twice, then the rear windshield was smashed in.

The Honda looked like it was made of tin, sounded and ran like it as well. I had a mechanic friend down the street, who I was constantly running to, banging on his door all hours of the day and night to try and get him to bail me out of my latest breakdown. It needed a new part and/or procedure every other week.

The Chevy, despite a hood-lock was popular for getting whole parts stolen, until one day the whole car was stolen from in front of my apartment. I got a call within 24 hours from the local police who gave me an address where I could recover it and when I saw what was left of it, I burst out laughing. It had been stripped to the bone of even the tiniest knob, button, wire, or switch—the complete chop shop treatment.

The Pontiac drank quarts of oil until the engine finally exploded. If cars are a punctuation to your life, the Pontiac was a period. And none of it would have happened if I could afford an operable car in the first place. But you've got to have one. After all, you may need to get to an audition.

AUDITIONS

The digital age has made live auditions for the most part a thing of the past. I loved live auditioning. I always felt employed whenever I had a few on the calendar. Auditions are a precious thing. They may be your only chance to act that week, so it's best to enjoy yourself. Why not? It's fun.

The script pages containing your character's lines are your "sides." In the digital age, sides are usually sent to you as an attachment. Before then, you were sometimes given the sides in advance or sometimes upon your arrival—in which case, it was a "Cold Reading." There was something about the immediacy of a cold reading that I always loved. I was good at it. It forced you to think on your feet. You learned to love the challenge of it, the sense of danger, the feel of a major league at bat; a chance to either swing for the fences or strike out; a skill to be constantly developed. Sometimes you read for a panel of live people, sometimes before a camera. In that case, tapes are then reviewed by producers at other locations.

At nearly every audition I went to, a scene played out in the waiting room that I witnessed a hundred times. Two actors, usually male, would run into each other and launch into a twisted little ritual.

Actor #1: Hey, how you doin'? Great to see you! *(What are YOU doing here? How did you get up on MY part?)*

Actor #2: Hey buddy! Great to see you too! *(Oh God, not this guy.)*

Actor #1: What have you been up to? *(Are you more successful than me?)*

Actor #2: Oh, I just wrapped a movie with _____. *(Yes, I am!)*

Actor #1: Oh yeah? I worked with him last year on _____. *(I already know him better than you do, which means I'm further along in my career than you are, so your job isn't such a big deal.)* Great director and a really nice guy. *Really* nice guy.

Actor #2: Yeah, he is. Isn't he? *(What an arrogant jerk.)*

NOTE: This one's a giveaway.
There *aren't* any really nice guys in Hollywood.

Actor #1: Hey, do you remember_____? *(I've been working longer than you.)*

The badminton match continues from here, usually too loudly for comfort and right up to the second their names are called. These guys see it as a social occasion, a networking opportunity. I was always amazed they had time for this. If it's a cold reading, you have whatever precious time is available before your reading to relax, study, concentrate, and preferably get the lines down so you don't have to glance at the script. On an in-person audition, if you are reading for a camera, depending upon who's behind it, you may have several takes worth of fun. In cases like this, it helps if you keep your cold reading chops up, so you can stretch yourself a little and use the opportunity to give them your very best take. There are few things worse than regretting a bad audition, so take your time to relax and ease yourself into it.

Another creature of this venue is a fellow I've identified as "The Guy." Who is he? The Guy thinks everyone has been waiting for him to arrive. The Guy has a bellowing, false laugh that you can hear from the other side of the room. He never stops talking from the second he arrives, and he laughs at everything. The Guy thinks that if he chats up the receptionist and impresses her with his schtick, that will help him get a job. He is so relentless; he barely has a human identity left. He drops names continuously in his non-stop monologue. He knows every celebrity personally. I got so familiar with The Guy, I could spot him across the room. And I mentioned him enough times that when I would come back from auditions, friends would ask, "Hey, was The Guy there?" Oh, yes indeed. He's *always* there.

The upside of the modern model of home-taping is you get to stay home. Also, you have the luxury of doing as many takes as you want to give them your best. Your finished product is then delivered to an online drop box. And the rest is out of your hands. Some you get. Some you don't.

Now, whether you like it or not, here comes the dreaded . . .

"<u>BELL CURVE OF AGONY</u>"

This is the period between your audition or call back and the time you hear whether or not you have been cast. No matter how old you are or how long you've been in the business, it never gets any easier. Not even a little bit. It goes roughly like this:

<u>Day 1</u> – You know it went well and you did your best. It feels like the odds are in your favor and you have a pretty good chance. It's a great job and an excellent credit to have.

<u>Day 2</u> – Holding steady and feeling good. You sure could use the money, but you can't be thinking that way. You find yourself doing things to keep your mind off it.

<u>Day 3</u> – The self-insulation phase. You figure if you don't get it, it's not the end of the world. It's just another job. You do wish they would just let you know and get it over with.

<u>Day 4</u> – You wake up angry and a little nauseous. You wonder what's taking them so long. You know you're perfect for this. Don't they know that? How much time do they need? You set an arbitrary bar for yourself to officially lose hope at noon tomorrow.

<u>Day 5</u> – At noon, it dawns on you that maybe they *haven't* made a final decision. There could still be an outside chance since there are so many people involved. No need for panic. You're good.

<u>Day 6</u> – Shit. Looks like you didn't get it. Goddam it. You

thought for sure you had this one in the bag. You hate show business and everyone in it.

Day 7 – You wonder if there's still a longshot? Maybe not everyone's weighed in on the final decision yet, huh?

Day 8 – All right, *fuck those people!* They're a bunch of scumbags and I'm not letting them ruin my life. Boy, aren't you pathetic, keeping your hopes up like that? Don't be such a dunce!

Day 9 and beyond – Well, you can find a hole to crawl into or you can pick up the jagged splinters of your shattered soul, remind yourself of reasons for living, and get your pummeled ego ready for another "bell curve of agony," because it's coming, kids. It's one of the few things in showbiz you can rely on.

Usually, if the producer is considering you, they will call your agent for a "Check Avail" which is a request to make sure there are no scheduling conflicts if they hire you. It doesn't always mean you have the job, but it's a good sign that you did something right even if you don't. But, if you do, hooray for you! You got a job! Now go have some fun.

I was auditioning at the Santa Monica Auditorium for a stage production of *The Boys in the Band.* During the reading, I thought it was going pretty well because the director seemed very attentive and involved, letting me do the entire scene several times. After the reading, he approached me with a big smile, moved in quite close, and touched my hip. "Listen," he said. "Me and some friends are having a pool party in Malibu, would you like to come?" He was so overt about it, I thought, there's got to be something wrong about this. This is an audition, man, not a nightclub. What if I was a woman? Would this be a #MeToo moment? I didn't want to rattle anybody, I just wanted to go home, so I thanked him and slipped through the lobby out into the street.

This is common. I'm sure at the same moment, the exact same thing was happening to a bunch of other actors of all genders in casting offices all over town. I know way too many actors who have run into situations like this. It's both a pain and an unfortunate acknowledged reality. Just passing along some information you should be aware of here.

On another occasion, getting sick of the laundry list of reasons for not getting jobs, I saw an audition notice for a British character in a stage production of a French farce. The notice said that they wanted an authentic British accent which I knew I could do. I figured I would do them one better and actually *be* a Brit. On the phone, setting up the time, I identified myself as Terry Rees Corbyn, a bloke in America for a bash at some auditions.

When I got there and met the producers, I let them know just how jolly good it was to meet such a smashing couple of chaps after only being stateside a fortnight. When they asked where I was born, I said I originally hailed from Dorset in the West Country but grew up in London. I also mentioned that if the lads were to cast me in their show, I would bloody well make a commitment to stay. I knew enough of London to chat it up about certain areas of the city—Hampstead, Westminster. It went over perfectly. I was expecting them to break out the tea and shepherd's pie. I could see they bought the persona, but would it translate into a job?

Might as well cut to the punchline on this one. In the finished production, they ended up casting a close friend of the company, a blonde completely Anglo-American guy with the phoniest attempt at a British accent you'll ever want to hear. They lied. Instead of casting an actor they thought was from Britain, they went with a guy they knew wasn't. Another lesson. Not everyone practices truth in advertising.

SCAMALOT

Because of the widespread murkiness about the way the industry functions, there has never been any shortage of elaborate schemes in Hollywood designed to separate actors from their money. I certainly fell for a bunch. Take your pick. Probably the most common is *The Casting Director's Showcase.* The way this works is a casting director from a TV production or one of the studios is paid to sit and watch an afternoon of scenes. The actors pay out of pocket to participate on the chance they will be "discovered" or at least called up to read for an existing show. The casting director is in no way obligated to actually do any of that. They can use the time to tell or teach the actors anything they want to. Or nothing at all. But they get paid anyway. This is a good way for casting directors to make money on the side, simply by virtue of their title. And a lot of them do it because their jobs don't really pay that much.

You have to admire the genius—and the balls—of this arrangement. They tell you right up front that there is not a shred of a guarantee of getting *any* work or even one audition out of it. How many businesses can you think of that take your money and promise you absolutely nothing in return? Casino gambling. And that's exactly what this is too. A chance to pull the lever on the one-armed bandit. And they're not misrepresenting anything. Over time, there have been a number of permutations of this setup, so I fell for it several times in a few different guises. Hope springs eternal. Some "forums" involve paying admission to hear some industry person spew for an hour. The first time I participated in one, the casting director spent most of his time just telling stories of things actors do that annoy him. "Don't do this people! *Please* don't do this." He spent a lot of time rolling his eyes and berating us as a group. People did get to perform their scene/monologue to a blank face and leave a pix/res. I vowed to be a little more skeptical next time.

The Actor's Center on Ventura Boulevard was in a building with large picture windows through which you could see three floors of people buzzing about, in and out of classrooms, sitting in mutual common reception areas reading the trades or standing in groups, chatting. From the street, it looked to be quite the showbiz hub of activity, smack dab in the middle of Studio City, walking distance to the CBS Studio Center. One day, with my bag of pictures, resumes, tapes, and scripts, I went to have a look. It had the appearance of a full-fledged showbiz college. They had classes in different subjects running all day in four different classrooms. I checked the schedule and signed up for one called *Inside the Casting Process*. Well, in the first five minutes, I realized that *The Actor's Center* was actually *The Casting Director's Showcase* delivered on an industrial scale, three floors full, all day long. Dinged yet again.

This casting director asked for everyone's picture and resume, which at least sounded promising, so I handed over mine. He then proceeded to go through the stack, holding up each person's picture one by one, critiquing it in front of the group. "Oh God no! You're completely obscured in shadow here. See? / That's not a good look for you. / Too much makeup here. / It's better in natural lighting. / That's not a good pose. It doesn't show your best side. / You don't need a high-fashion makeup shot ladies, just one that looks like you!"

What a pissy character, I thought. So, accepting that I'd been had, I figured they already have my money, I will not let this little shit publicly humiliate me. So, while he wasn't looking, I sneaked over to the stack and pulled my picture before he could get to it. Then came the acting part, or according to this prick, trial by fire. He brought up each of us, one at a time, handed us a script of a romantic male/female love scene and read opposite each of us, reading the woman's part. Then... surprise, he systematically ripped each performance to pieces in the exact same manner he did our pictures. Watching each victim going up before me made me steel myself inside, mustering all my acting chops to fight this guy with pure acting and nothing else. I *DARE* you to fuck with me!

Finally, I came up, sat opposite him and locked my eyes on him with a look that said ... *love!* I love you! I need you more than anything! You are my world and my joy and I couldn't live without you! It was just for a fleeting second, but I saw him do a small double take. Touchdown. Caught you off guard, asshole. At this point, it became a battle of wits. He couldn't destroy me because I was too much in love with him. I could see an idea pop into his head. "All right," he said. "Now you read the woman's part." He didn't ask that of any other actor. He sat back and folded his arms. Without a beat, I found the broken-hearted woman and brought her out in full regalia, tears and all. He fumbled with the script a minute looking for the man's dialogue. When we finished, he was completely silent. I won. He didn't open his mouth at all. Within a few minutes, he started thanking everyone for coming and dismissed everybody. I decided to go for broke, so I lingered and approached him when the place was almost empty.

> "I showed you what I can do. Can you bring me up on your show?" I asked.
> "Oh," he said. "We've just finished casting the season."
> "How about an agent referral?" I asked.
> "Oh no no, I couldn't do that." he said, shaking his head.
> "But you could," I said. No response.
> "What you mean is, you'd rather not. Right?" He busied himself, collecting some papers, putting them in his bag and heading for the door.
> "I'm sorry, I really do have to go. Thanks for coming. Maybe I'll see you again."

I'll let you guess if that happened.

"It would mean so much to me if you came along," she said on the phone. It came as a pleasant surprise that something I could do would mean *anything* to her. So, naturally I had to go. Cindy was a very attractive actress. The event she wanted me to attend with her was called the *Actor's Group* which sounded relatively fun. Actors group. I thought fine, if nothing else I'll spend a little time with some other actors.

The event took place in a large hotel conference center. Tables with literature out in the lobby were staffed with actors as well. Everyone was extraordinarily friendly and greeted us with huge smiles. I was handed a name tag in a plastic holder that you pin to your jacket or shirt. We walked into the auditorium and found seats among the rows of folding chairs. People recognized each other and chatted about the industry. Now, I admit that I was so jazzed to be in Cindy's company, I really could have cared less about whatever we were about to hear. So, I figured I might as well enjoy it.

A loud voiced, smiling woman in a red blazer jacket jumped on stage and welcomed everyone, for which she received thunderous applause. I momentarily thought she was a famous actress I was unaware of. I must have looked confused because Cindy leaned over and explained that everyone applauds that way as part of their welcoming ritual. Uh-oh, I thought. Artificial enthusiasm. Even though that's what actors do, I began to bristle.

There are few things in this world that piss me off more than groupthink. Of any kind. It just brings out the raging punk in me. I want to punch everyone in the face and burn the whole place down. Of course, even though young men have been known to go to much greater lengths in the name of getting close to a woman, I should have warned Cindy, because I think I was doing a bad job of concealing my disgust. The moderator lady marked up a chalk board with lists of words, diagrams, and little cartoons. The crowd reacted to everything with laughter, applause, and cheers no matter what she said or did; they had enough energy to fuel an ocean liner.

Then, it was time for the testimonials. A pretty, red-haired girl stood up to more applause. She seemed to be a favorite among the group. "Life was a constant struggle. I couldn't get an agent. I was running out of money," she said. "My boyfriend had just broken up with me and I was really feeling pretty hopeless. Then, a friend brought me to the *Actor's Group,* and I truly couldn't believe what began to happen in my life. After about a month, I got signed by a major agency, I did three different TV shows, and scored a national Coke commercial!" Thunderous applause. The moderator lady smiled.

"You see what a change of attitude can do?" she said. "The only real limits are the ones you place on yourself!" Then, a dark-haired young man stood up to more applause and gave us a similar scenario about his career. "I learned how to shift my entire outlook and take a whole new approach to the industry," he said. "The change is so monumental, there's no describing it in words." Maybe not for him. I can think of a few.

Finally, someone mentioned the $500 fee that comes with membership in the group. "Don't let the $500 be the thing that stands between you and your success," the moderator said. "You know you'll be making ten times that much once you let your career happen. Most of the time you will find that you may be your own worst obstacle. Get out of your own way."

Something about that last suggestion registered with me because memory tells me I quickly made for the doors. I honestly don't remember what I said to Cindy, if anything. I just remember an intense heat, like my skin was burning off and I had to run to put the flames out. After that, I don't recall seeing Cindy again, so I guess I wish her the best, wherever she may be. So far, I haven't seen her in a national Coke commercial. For her sake, I hope someday I do.

Footnote: *The Actor's Group* was a subset of the *EST* movement of the 1970's. In the 90's it was known as *The Forum*. I found out years later that the line Cindy said to me had been fed to her verbatim. "It would mean so much to me if you came along" is exactly what you are instructed to say. These people understand human behavior extremely well. They know what will reach people on a subconscious level. What better way to bring people in than through the promise of fulfilling a close friend's wishes? In fact, you may get so caught up in it and the relationships you form in the group, you might even forget they took your money.

DIGRESSION

By this point, I know what some of you must be thinking. So rather than have it linger in the ether and trickle out in pieces, why don't I save you some time and just cram all of it into one paragraph. Ok? So here we go . . .

"Well, maybe it's *your* fault Dave. You ever think of that? Huh? You think you're so special? Maybe you're just a fucking loser. Maybe you didn't make it because you're just *not that talented*. Did you ever consider that? Huh? Oh, so you gotta work for a living? Well, boo- hoo! Things are tough all over. Nobody *owes* you a career, pal. What if it's all just sour grapes and you're just not really that good an actor *or* writer? How about *that?* You had a big, fat head and a big, fat overblown ego and thought you'd leave everyone else in the dust, but guess what? The joke is on you, asshole. You're the one who got left behind and that's the cold, hard fact. Your worst nightmare has come true and you didn't even notice. So, deal with it, shmuck. Go write a book."

Ok? There it is. Did I leave anything out? Good.

So, moving right along . . .

GOOD LUCK

Darrel was a good looking young black actor who I met while in rehearsal for a showcase. He was fairly new to acting but took it very seriously and we talked a lot about the industry. At the time, he had just signed with a reputable agent. I was invited over to his house one night where I met his wife Kerry, a stunning blonde woman who seemed to really believe in Darrel and his career. We all stood chatting on their backyard patio for a while. My gaze kept drifting between the beautiful appointments of the house and those of his wife. The house was a spacious, classy home with nice art on the walls.

Man, I thought. Some guys truly do get all the luck. Look at Darrel. New in town with a gorgeous house, a beautiful wife and on top of that, he had just scored the gig of a lifetime—a recurring role on a major network soap opera. The role required that he move to New York where the show taped. Kerry was not happy about having to leave a place they just moved to but was certainly ready for the new opportunity. That's the way it happens sometimes. So, this was their farewell get together and I wished them all the best knowing, selfishly I would really miss hanging out with them.

While Darrel went to New York to be a soap opera star, I returned to my menial job at the law firm, sorting mail and stocking supplies. In my mind's eye, I saw Darrel strolling through Times Square or getting in makeup down at 30 Rock. Well, it turns out it didn't stay in my mind's eye for long because one day while pushing a mail cart around the floors at my usual clip, I saw out of the corner of my eye Darrel in close-up on the TV in the kitchen. Turns out a few of the secretaries watched the show regularly. I parked my mail cart against the outside hallway and sat down to watch for a while. Darrel looked great. His lighting was perfect. His character was the love interest opposite the ingénue in a big romantic scene, complete with dramatic music. Good going, Darrel, I thought. Do that job, buddy!

A few weeks later, I was shopping at a Walgreen's drug store when Darrel appeared again, this time on the cover of a soap opera fan magazine, which I picked up to read. The magazine contained all kinds of made-up storylines, supposedly revealing the "inside scoop" on Darrel's life. They didn't mention his wife of course. There were pictures of him and his leading lady posing all over Central Park in different clothes, lounging in a boat, holding hands at a café, strolling on the waterfront. Wow. Darrel was now fully inside the machine.

Because of the physical distance, I fell out of touch with Darrel and began to adjust myself to the fact that I may never see him again, except on TV. That can happen as people's careers diverge, so in that respect, it made me sad. A good bit of time passed and at one point, I noticed that

Darrel's character had either been discontinued or written out of the show. It gave me pause, but life goes on. In the meantime, my fantasies of flight kept me going through my workdays.

On the weekends, I loved to go walking on Santa Monica Beach. One particularly foggy afternoon, I was groping along the seashore, water washing over my feet, when out of the mist comes Darrel, walking slowly toward me. He didn't see me at first because he walked with his head down, hands in his pockets.

"Hey buddy!" I called. "What brings you to the edge of the world?"

He seemed glad to see me, but there was clearly something wrong. I asked him how Kerry was which launched him into a monologue that kept us walking for a good hour. He told me the entire story. He had gone to New York where he and Kerry found a place and settled into a lifestyle that involved him being picked up by limousine every day, brought to the studio and back home every night. He told me he cleared $200,000 the first year.

Now the plot twist. Unbeknownst to him, Kerry had been spending at about the same rate he was earning. So, by the end of his contract, he was broke and unemployed. Then, she divorced him once the revenue stream dried up. So here he was, back in LA with no job, no money, no wife, and no house. He indicated even his agent situation was iffy. Talk about a Hollywood ending. He was famous for eight months and then it stopped. Our paths crossed a few more times and I eventually lost touch with him somewhere out in the vast grid of Los Angeles. It's like he turned around and drifted back into the mist from which he had emerged. I will always remember Darrel because nothing is ever what it seems in showbiz. The grass is always greener in fantasyland. It also made me a bit wary of marriage.

In a final twist, the last I heard of him, he had changed preferences from women to men, which made sense to me. I hope Darrel found love again and some money too. They're a little scarce down there in LA.

ACTING

So, what is all this *acting* stuff anyway? What is "The Method?" Is that the best way to learn acting? Who the hell is Stanislavski? Do you have to read those books? Aren't actors just a bunch of exhibitionists? Here's a fundamental question for any actor: Why are you doing this? What are you really after? Are you in it for the money? For the attention? Are you trying to prove something to yourself or someone else? It's impossible to discuss acting without first talking about art.

You walk into an art gallery filled with different paintings and sculptures. You have different reactions to different pieces. Some really draw you in, others may shock or repulse you, and others you may not notice at all. Some may be visually striking, others colorful, evocative or moody, some comedic or ironic, but notice how your limbic system responds to the images reflexively, immediately upon viewing them? By the end of the day, you may have experienced a full range of emotions and responses. All of this because a few people smeared some paint on some canvasses or built sculptures out of clay, wood, or whatever else they could find. Your subconscious and your life experiences fill in the blanks.

If you step back, you can see the power being thrown around here. Even if a certain image makes you recoil, the artist was nonetheless effective at evincing that response. Art encompasses the entirety of human experience. So that makes it something both awesome and delicate, something to be nurtured and treated with care. I believe the same applies to an actor's work on the stage. I was blessed to have had many great coaches who inspired me to keep pushing the bar higher. And above all to enjoy it.

The philosophy of acting I absorbed from all of them involve a process of consciously elevating the craft at every moment, cherishing it as a thing of value. You have a massive landscape waiting for you to carve your little niche in, which will only be as boring or as thrilling as you decide it will be. One thing is for certain, if *you* don't think it's important, your audience certainly won't. Your work is only as special as you decide it is. There's an element of the miraculous here. Every performance has the potential for genuine magic, an emotional spark that resonates significantly, even if just for a single audience member. Respect and defer to that. It's much bigger than you are. You are the vessel, carrying and translating words into action and emotion.

So, what about "The Craft" "The Method" and all that stuff? Ok, well let's have a quick look at all that stuff, my fellow actors. Here's my best shot at making it not completely boring: Konstantin Stanislavski (1863-1938) was the premiere Russian actor/director of his day. He co-founded the famous Moscow Art Theatre which brought the plays of Anton Chekhov and Maxim Gorky to the attention of the world. He staged a wide range of classical Russian and European Productions that toured the world.

The reason his name comes up all the time is that he is credited as the "father" of method acting mostly because he was the first to ever identify the concept of "subtext" in drama, the idea of a "through-line" for a character's development. In fact, he was the first to create a diagram illustrating how the motivations of a character form a process. If you've ever seen his diagram, it looks like a pair of lungs, which to me is appropriate, because nothing helps build a character like breathing.

He eventually synthesized his ideas in the book *An Actor Prepares* which is regarded as seminal reading. When his touring company came to America, a very young Lee Strasberg attended the performances and was consumed with what he saw. Years later at the *Group Theatre* he founded in New York, Strasberg, along with Sanford Meisner and Stella Adler, furthered Stanislavski's ideas through instruction and scene study. Today, they are all regarded as the chief practitioners of "The Method." Now, here's where it spread out. When the *Group Theatre* disbanded in 1940, Meisner adapted his training with Strasberg into his own "Meisner Technique" which he taught at the *Neighborhood Playhouse* and later at *The Actors Studio* alongside director, Elia Kazan who, of course, eventually brought it to Hollywood. Marlon Brando's performance as Stanley Kowalski in Kazan's film version of *A Streetcar Named Desire* is considered a landmark example of method acting on screen.

So, to bring all this back home, when it comes to the individual actor, I've always felt that we have the benefit of all these great artistic minds to draw from. You don't have to choose. I've never seen a need for disagreement between schools of thought. There's always been plenty of chatter about the virtues and merits of "The Method" versus fill-in-the-blank acting style. The mission is the same—a believable performance. Every actor synthesizes what they have learned, melding techniques and ideas into a series of practices they are comfortable with. Beyond that, I don't see that there's much mystery to it.

There has also been controversy regarding certain practices actors use to prepare. Brando, DeNiro, Hoffman, and others have been known to undertake radical weight-loss or gain as well as subject themselves to certain experiences in the name of furthering their understanding of a character, such as sleeping in the street to play a homeless person or going to jail to play a prisoner. As eccentric as many of these actors' choices may seem, I can never fault an actor for whatever ritual they employ to get the needed result. Acting is a very personal, internal process. So, even though some may cause an eyeroll in the name of this, when the camera rolls, if the moment is truthful, that's what matters and what remains.

I cherry picked my way through my actor's training like I'm sure most actors do. Even now, I still use a few back pocket "tricks" that I learned at ACT, such as "sense memory," a basic technique of naturalism. When studying this, we all sat in circles holding our hands out over an imaginary flame. If you concentrate hard enough, you can spur your subconscious to remember what being burned feels like, so when you withdraw your hand, you actually feel heat. Things like that can become easy over time.

Throw all of that into your brain salad, then salt and pepper with ideas and art you admire. I perused Stanislavski as well as Uta Hagen's *Respect for Acting* (1973) which was a good basic read about actors at work. She broke down many basic tenets of acting without getting too intellectual. As a performer, I understand that *too much* character analysis can get in the way of the spontaneity an actor requires. It's important to do your basic research to understand your character and then, at some point, leave it be and engage your body and emotions for the process of "being" the character.

During a trip to Ireland, a friend and I shuttled over to London to see some West End Theatre and found ourselves near Shakespeare's original *Globe Theatre* on the Thames River. Adjacent to the lobby was a beautiful little museum illustrating the entire history of the English-speaking theatre through miniature dioramas—magnificently detailed artist's renderings of different costumes, sets and props. That, plus the guided tour of the theater itself left me with a bracing sense of the immensity and breadth of creativity that preceded us. Learning the real history of what actors do cannot help but enrich your understanding. If you ever find your way there, it's humbling to consider what's gone before and whatever small contribution you can make to this history.

Oh, one footnote on art . . .

DAVID HERN

THE VAN GOGH QUESTION

What really constitutes success or failure? There are actors
and artists who may have created some piece of brilliant
work, only to never work again. Some have worked a lot
and made a fortune without ever creating anything of note.
The highest grossing movie or actor is always the
newsworthy part, but many films that are now considered
classics brought lukewarm box office on their initial
release. Well, I've always wondered, what about the Van
Gogh Question? It is widely known that Vincent Van Gogh,
the Dutch painter, only sold a single painting in his entire
life. He struggled with severe depression and psychotic
episodes and over his lifetime was moved in and out of
different asylums. He drank and smoked heavily, suffered
from hallucinations and delusions, and in a famous
episode, severely wounded his right ear with a knife. For
much of his life, he lived on the edge of poverty and was
largely supported by his older brother, Theo, who
provided for him financially and emotionally up until
Vincent's premature death at age 37.

So, was Van Gogh a success or a failure? By all accounts, he
was considered a vagrant madman and his physical life on
this planet was clearly tortured. But, in the window of
history, he is regarded as one of the most revered and
talented artists of his age and his work is emulated to this
day. Deep emotional resonance and truth were the key
ingredients. And madness. They all collide in his art.
Several of his works are among the most expensive
paintings to have *ever* been sold. There is a museum in

Amsterdam that bears his name and contains many of his pieces that are now considered priceless.

John Kennedy Toole, the renowned author of the classic novel *A Confederacy of Dunces*, never knew literary success at all. Even though he was regarded as a brilliant wit, a prestigious college professor, and an exceptional academic, he could not get his novel published. After trying for decades and even after exhaustive re-writes, he was ultimately rejected by Simon & Schuster. Shortly afterward, he fell into a deep depression that ended in suicide. His book was published 11 years after his death from a manuscript he left behind. He won the Pulitzer Prize for fiction posthumously in 1981. So, success or failure? And why does Dave keep asking that?

The Van Gogh Question doesn't have a clear answer. Or rather, it has as many answers as people, depending on your values. It's kind of a litmus test. An investment banker would have had no interest in Vincent during his lifetime but would certainly line up outside Sotheby's Auction House for his works today. I guess in the end, art transcends time because it only actually exists inside human consciousness. That's where the *experience* of art happens. And you can't put a dollar value on that.

MAKE WAY FOR UNICORNS

One year as summer approached, I realized I was rapidly running out of money and food stamps. So once again began the dreary enterprise of looking for work. After a few weeks, I had an interview for a low-level clerical job at a publishing company. The manager who interviewed me was pleasant enough and showed me around the office which gave me the impression that I was probably in the running. By the end of the interview, he offered me the job and asked if I could start Monday.

Naturally, the parents were delighted. But inside I dreaded embarking on another long stretch of office life where everything is exactly the same, just re-fitted with a new location and set of co-workers. The next day, returning from breakfast, I picked up a message from the *Unicorn Players*, a troupe I had auditioned for the previous week offering me a job with their touring children's theatre company for a five-month contract performing on the road.

Well, I thought, let's see now... an unending life of fluorescent lit drudgery in a non-descript office all day *OR* five months on the road as an employed actor. It wasn't a hard choice. The hard part was explaining it to the parents, who thought I was losing my mind and blowing my future up. For better or worse, I called the publishing company HR manager back and politely declined the position, truthfully citing "other employment opportunities." And so began my first experience of survival as an actor. And it was wonderful. Just the sheer thrill of existence on the planet as a working actor. Of course, every acting gig ends, but it still felt pretty sensational.

The show was a one-act version of *The Ransom of Red Chief*, an O. Henry short story about two inept criminals who kidnap the 3-year-old son of a wealthy landowner and hold him for ransom. The adaptation wasn't bad and was chock full of great opportunities for broad old-style slapstick. In the story, the child hostage loves to play little Indian chief, running around with a tomahawk screaming all day long. He pushes his two captors to the edge of sanity and to the point where they end up paying the father to take him back. I was introduced to my other two cast mates—Chuck and Mike. Chuck was a huge, roly-poly guy who could cross his eyes pretty well which is always a hit with kids. He played my partner in crime and we looked funny together—a Laurel and Hardy kind of match-up. Mike, who I called Mikey, was hired to play the little boy and looked the part. Small, thin, and gangly, he could easily be mistaken for a child. My character, Sam, was supposed to be the "brains" of the bumbling pair but was of course just as stupid as his partner. I opted for a sloppy New York accent. We rehearsed the show for a month, which went fairly smoothly.

Then, the brave band of players—Chuck, Mike and myself, three complete strangers— hit the road to live and work together for five months. Our wood framed canvas set pieces folded up to fit neatly in the back of a van, which transported us along with our props, costumes, and makeup—a mobile troupe of goofballs coming to your town.

Altogether, a pretty good deal, I thought. The gigs were all pre-scheduled in locations up and down the state of California, from the Oregon border down to San Isidro. Our accommodations were all pre-booked through a commercial motel chain. Since the chain's rooms are identical, it felt like we were staying in the same room with a different window view each day.

I grew to enjoy wandering the sickly yellow light of Motel 6 hallways, looking for the ice and vending machine cove. It was familiar, calming. They'll never know how much one actor found their rooms to be "just like home." Some of the performance locations were so remote, we wondered A.) if the office gave us the right address and B.) if the people we were going to perform for had ever seen any theatre at all. We played in school auditoriums and gymnasiums, churches (on altars) and one room schoolhouses in the middle of nowhere. On several of the cold mornings out on the plains, we made our way to locations driving through mist so thick, the roads were barely visible. At the motel one morning, somewhere in the remotest farmlands, I woke up in a groggy state, stumbled to the picture window, threw open the drapes and came face to face with a huge cow, his massive unblinking face looking right at me with a frozen stare. All I could do was stand there and marvel at the size of this animal's face. Here's an important lesson I learned that day. Never try to stare down a cow. You will lose.

Chuck, in addition to playing my partner, was also hired as the tour manager, responsible for the payroll paperwork and reporting info back to the tour office in LA. On the first leg of our journey, we stopped for lunch at the first of many Denny's restaurants in tiny towns off the freeways of the state. About halfway through our meal, Chuck turned and frowned at me. "You're disgusting, do you know that?" he said. I had no idea what was happening. "What's wrong?" I asked." "You're a disgusting eater," he said. "I can't stand watching you eat!" Not knowing quite how to respond to this, I looked at him quizzically. After a moment, he got up and moved to another table on the far side of the restaurant. I turned to Mike. "Oh well, Mikey, it looks like us two." Mikey didn't seem to be perturbed by this and just kept eating. After the meal, we met outside back at the van. Chuck announced that he didn't want to room with either of us. So, from that moment forward, every place we booked had Mikey and me in one room and Chuck in the other. Also, every meal had Mikey and me at one table and Chuck at another. Ok, I thought. We're still employed.

Up at six, we would meet at the van by seven, hit a breakfast joint by seven thirty and off to the gig. Every morning in the cold, Chuck would address us like a drill sergeant. "Ok, we're going to do the show at the schoolhouse and then we have to go *BACK* to St. Michael's for the show tonight." This, even though we all had the printed schedule in advance. During most of the long rides, I read William Goldman's *Adventures in the Screen Trade*, one of the best books on screenwriting ever written and every night after the show and dinner, I would work on my first screenplay in the motel room while Mikey watched television. I had resolved to have a first draft done by the end of the tour. It really felt pretty fantastic to be acting all day and writing at night. In spite of the weird triangle of personalities, we pulled off every show on time and usually with appreciative audiences. I got to hear rooms full of children laughing every day. Not a bad way to earn a living. Much joy to be found.

Mikey had a pale, sickly pallor most of the time. In the room at night, he would feed himself junk food, polishing off whole packages of chocolate Donette's, Twizzlers, and Junior Mints. Sometimes, I could hear him coughing or even lightly choking in his sleep. I could only attribute this to the sheer volume of his sugar intake. Then one night Mikey talked at length about a movie starring Christie Baylor.

At the time, Christie Baylor was a young star of romantic teen movies who had been a child star on a long running TV show. I also knew she was gay, which ran counter to her screen persona of the time which needed to be maintained, sadly for her. I mentioned the irony of this to Mikey. What I didn't know was that I had just destroyed Mikey's dreams. He began sweating, trembling, and crying as he pulled away from me with a look of horror in his eyes. "No, she's not! She's *NOT!*" he hollered at me and stormed out of the room. Great, I thought. Now I've alienated Mikey too. Am I going to be alone for the rest of the tour? A few hours later, he silently returned to the room and went to bed. I was genuinely relieved and felt even a bit grateful. No sense ruining a good working relationship over a person neither of us knew.

By the middle of the tour, Chuck began to elevate his status to director. "You're up there taking your 'method' pauses and the show is dragging!" he yelled at me one afternoon. Seeing as things had been going fairly smoothly, it felt like Chuck was looking for a controversy. Either that or maybe he missed the delightful company of Mikey and me after walling himself off for the entire tour. "Look Chuck," I said. "The show was already directed before we hit the road and I think we're going over pretty well." Chuck looked at me like he was waiting for something. "I'll keep the pace up, ok?" I said, hoping that would satisfy him. He walked off in a huff. Later that night, for reasons I can't remember, things escalated to the point where Chuck threatened to punch me out and I threatened to abandon the tour if he didn't back off. Mikey threatened to sue me, but then reversed himself and played peacemaker between Chuck and me. Thanks to him, life snapped back to relative normal so we could finish the job.

By the three-quarter mark of the tour, I think it's safe to say that we were all pretty sick of one another and were eager and ready to never see each other again. We had one grand finale performance scheduled at a large church in San Francisco. The setting was appropriate as by that point, we sure needed some prayers. In the middle of the show, one of the larger set pieces toppled, tore its canvas, and fell to the ground. We managed to rescue the scene and finish the show, then load up the broken set into the van and head home. But I always felt that it was providential in some way and symbolic of our broken tour that needed to wrap up. Like they said in Vaudeville, sometimes you need to take a hint and leave the stage before you get the hook.

FOR THE GRACE

The road made me aware of something. Have you ever noticed when travelling, regardless of where you may go, as you are drifting off to sleep, if you listen very carefully you can hear someone hollering off in the distance? I find that strangely comforting. No matter where you are, you can always count on there being a crazy guy out there screaming into the night. It's almost like he follows you from city to city, keeping you company.

I could be wrong but in LA, I think *he's* got company. I'm sure I heard people of all stripes out there making different noises. More than that, I saw more amazing human behavior there than in any other place. A lot in showbiz and a lot right on the street. Around the corner from the block where I lived, there was a crack house at one end and a corner strip mall where hookers hung out at the other. A skinny dark-haired girl was usually cruising back and forth on the boulevard. After a while, her routine became clear. She would sell herself for cash, then walk down to the crack house to spend it. Then after smoking it up, she would head back up the street to hustle for more cash to go back and score again. I never saw her anywhere else in the city. That block was her beat and universe. And you could tell where she was in the arc from which direction she was walking. Left for hustling, right for drugs. I wondered how she got herself stuck in this loop. Where did she come from?

I think the winner of the most stunning street behavior though goes to something I saw in downtown LA in the middle of a bright, sunny day. It was brutally hot at the bustling street fair with people milling about everywhere. I was running an errand for work in my business suit, making my way through the crowd and noticed a very old woman wearing a loose-fitting floral dress carrying a waxy, partially crushed movie-theater cup. She leaned over and into a squatting posture, peed into the cup under her skirt, then turned and threw the contents at passersby. It took me a moment to believe what I was seeing. She did this several times and with such purpose and intensity, it was astounding. Like it was her job.

I think these people remain in my consciousness because I always knew inside that, despite my goddam business suit, I was also just a paycheck away from homelessness and poverty. These people remind us of the primal in us. What if you had to play a character like this? As overtly crazed and dysphoric as they may seem, as an actor, you owe them some honesty, not a caricature. They were all once children, just like you. You have more things in common than you probably would like to believe. Actors, take note. You have much to be grateful for.

THE GREAT TOMMY P

After a few years of hanging around *Nosotros*, I had become kind of the semi-unofficial white guy of the Latino theatre company. I was always there. My friends and cohorts were Puerto Rican, Mexican, Black, and Middle Eastern. At one point, it hit me that I could bring the writer in me to the task of writing a play for what was already a great assortment of people and characters—my theatre crew. Let's try and put us all to work. I realized I had to be the one to bring it about.

So, I commenced a nightly writing routine and after a few months produced a draft of *In the Birdcage*—the story of a young trainee bail bondsman who ends up running the office for a day. Being a trainee, he quickly loses control of the proceedings and finds himself effectively held hostage in his own office by a pair of angry customers. I tried my best to do well by each of the characters in terms of giving them prominent scenes and some good laugh lines. The first raw table reading went extraordinarily well. Lots of laughs and a sense of potential. I began to get excited about the possibilities. It seemed we might have something here. I did some polishing and kicked out another draft.

My friends and I started brainstorming on how to present it as a staged reading one night at the playhouse. We decided to take an ad out in *Drama Logue* (LA's industry rag) to hold auditions for casting the remaining open roles, and then think in terms of rehearsal and publicity. The thinking was that if we could invite industry professionals, it could be a good showcase for all of us. The audition process was interesting and a bit crazy. Here we all were, scraping away at our individual careers, and then purely because we took an ad out in *Drama Logue* and held public auditions, suddenly a mass of *other* actors were subjugating themselves before us trying to be noticed. Pretty quick role reversal.

One of the key parts we were casting was the rotund Irish owner of the business, Jack Muldowney, a crusty older bail bondsman with a huge gut and an Archie Bunker-ish demeanor. One actor, Bill Hatch, had bulging eyes and a particularly funny rhythm to his speech that I knew would be perfect. We found the other actors we were looking for and scheduled a final staged reading with the full cast. Now, between the two readings, one of my friends had given the script to a television producer primarily known for a late-night syndicated horror show. Tommy P, as he was known, had been an industry producer/director for a while. Several of my friends sang his praises and were very excited that he was interested enough in the script to attend our one remaining audition. They said he might be interested in developing it as a potential TV series. Sounded pretty good to me and I resolved to make him feel as welcome as possible.

The day of the audition, in the early afternoon we were all watching a young actor slog through a scene timidly, but with determination. Suddenly, I heard a loud voice talking right over the proceedings. "Yeah, yeah, yeah, where is this kid . . . Dave?"

Everyone looked toward the door and there was Tommy P, dressed in a huge, fur-lined overcoat with an attractive woman on his arm. He presented as a hybrid of an Elvis impersonator and a motorhome salesman. The woman had the look of a gangster moll, complete with the chewing gum and thoroughly bored look in her eyes. "Yeah, now what are you trying here?" he said, moving into the room, mingling, and chatting. Probably without much tact, I tried to get the guy onstage to wrap it up. I introduced myself to Tommy and his girl who didn't seem to look directly at anyone.

Everyone else began to leave as my core group and Tommy huddled in the bleacher seats of the playhouse. In all honesty, a great deal of what was said that day is pretty fuzzy, but a few moments stayed with me. When we talked about casting, the role of Vicky came up. As written, Vicky is a short, white albino prostitute with a loud mouth. Tommy, put his arm out and herded me away from the group, out of earshot. "You see this girl?" he said with a grin. "Well, let me tell you, *this* girl is a hooker! I know what I'm talking about, you know what I mean?" I pondered a response. On the one hand, this woman was tall and brunette, not at all like the character of Vicky. In addition, there's a difference between a hooker and an actress *playing* a hooker. Didn't seem to matter to Tommy. "Ok," I said. That's something we could consider."

After a few long war stories about the industry, it became obvious Tommy didn't like me much and I guess I returned the favor. We couldn't have been more opposite characters. At some point, he began to talk about money. "I'll give you five thousand," he said. "Half upfront and the rest after we sign the show." He also made it clear that I would in no way be involved in the casting, writing, or any other aspect of the production. In my head, I partly thought he was kidding. "You mean, that's it?" I asked. He was offering me five thousand dollars to go away—to turn over my work to him with no further say about any aspect of what happened to it. And no percentage of anything the show might generate later.

This left me in one of the weirdest positions I've ever found myself. Completely outnumbered and checkmated by my friends who were obviously sold on the idea and enamored of Tommy's "clout." One of my friends told me he thought I was insane not to "turn the whole thing over to Mister Tommy P!" I recall hearing another saying, slightly angrily "Oh, you think you've got to be some kind of fucking *artist*?" On the one hand, my gut knew that whatever Tommy P did with my play, it would end up with no resemblance to what I wrote, and I would never see another penny. On the other hand, I certainly wouldn't have been the last guy to sell himself out in the name of getting over in Hollywood. In the end, despite the entreaties of my compatriots, I just couldn't hand my baby over to be pimped out on Hollywood Boulevard.

A week or so later came the day of the reading. Invitations had been mailed out and we had received a decent number of RSVP's, including a few reputable industry people. Also, chilled champagne and hors d'oeuvres had been ordered and arrived just as we all were gathering at the playhouse.

As we entered and began setting up, I saw there were no stage lights up, just the fluorescent work lights, so I asked one of our crew to go up in the booth, dim the house, and bring up the stage. It turned out no one had a key to the booth. A few frantic calls were made to others on the playhouse staff, but this being a Sunday, to no avail. We were stuck basically, facing the reality of performing under that pale, headache inducing light with no air conditioning either. Well, I thought. Buck up. At least we have a playhouse and an audience arriving. Of course, as they did you could see them enter the scene with some level of confusion as they took their seats.

Well, as the reading began, all I can say is that for some reason—suddenly—_everybody_ _choked_, myself included. We all stank. In public. Bill Hatch, who had been so brilliant in the early readings with his naturally funny voice, suddenly scrunched up his face and voice, trying to create some artificially "comic character." Nothing worked. The timing was so off, even the sure-fire laugh lines died. As for me, I felt like Nero, fiddling away. At one point my gaze drifted to the audience, and I could see that the single most important audience member, a producer who I had tried so hard to get to attend, was drifting off to sleep. The rest of the crowd seemed to be gazing over at the food trays and champagne in plain sight stage left.

As a writer, it was interesting to note how the fluorescent light, like an X-Ray machine, revealed all the flaws in the play itself—the most obvious one being my own character, Ollie Greenberg, the junior bondsman. It became noticeable that I had been so focused on the characters created for my cast that I neglected to really flesh out Ollie. He had no real identity or understandable motivation. Oops. It's easier to write for others. You can see them. So here I was playing a poorly defined character, watching everything else crumble around me, wincing inside at every flaw, every missed beat.

When the torture mercifully ended, the audience descended on the food, devoured everything in sight and quickly disappeared, which I would have done too, but I was responsible for all this. I have no memory of how the night eventually ended, but life did go on and return to normal, meaning back to the day job. I worked at *Nosotros* a few more times, but never wrote any further drafts of *In the Birdcage.* Today, it sits on my shelf like an abandoned child with a club foot. It was the one and only time I tried to write a play to fit a cast of characters instead of casting characters to fit a play. Since then, I've written others that are far more viable.

If I am fully honest with myself, all these years later, I guess I might as well have taken Tommy's stinking five grand and used it to cover a couple of months' rent. The worst that could have happened to the play was nothing, which is what happened anyway. So, if I had sold it, it would have been nothing—plus five thousand dollars. I guess I was trying to be some kind of fucking artist.

WRITING

"Speaking Frankly means saying things a guy named Frank would say."

(I don't remember who said this)

I love writing. And in Hollywood, I found it just as impossible to do for a living as acting. Now that we've been through a few elements of the Hollywood paradigm, I'm sure you may recall reading a story or two about some TV actress in a magazine that goes "... and then she came to Hollywood and started off by doing commercials." This kind of reporting always irritated me because it intentionally omits so much. What are they saying? She got off the bus, walked to a set, and started filming a commercial? It doesn't work like that.

Similarly, trying to be a produced stage or screenwriter is just as fraught with much of the same roadblocks and exclusionary structures that actors face. You need a literary agent, you need membership in the Writers Guild of America, and you need bunches and bunches of luck, mostly at getting people to read your script at all. So, rather than slosh through the same rigmarole, let's talk instead about a huge literary success story—Harry Potter. Most people are familiar with the uphill battles and numerous rejections author J.K. Rowling encountered along the way. Then, of course, her incredible success that created an entire marketing universe of everything from movies, video and board games to lunch boxes, T-shirts, and frozen pops.

When I first heard of her early struggles, I was impressed with her tenacity, but I wanted to drill down one level further. Something was missing from the story here. First of all, every literary agent has a standing policy of not accepting "unsolicited" manuscripts. All that means is "we will not read anything we didn't ask you for." Rowling, like every writer, was once "unsolicited." So, this means she must have had a freak accident. Just like I did to get into SAG. Something must break your way. Most agencies immediately throw the manuscripts they didn't ask for on a stack for returns or for the incinerator. Well, it turns out that is indeed what happened. She submitted her manuscript to several agents and sure enough, it ended up on the "unsolicited" pile. Now, for some reason that we *don't* know, one day, at one agency, one agent happened to look momentarily over at the manuscript pile just long enough to pick it up and crack it open. Now, can we freeze frame and zoom in here? Nobody would have ever known about it if nobody ever opened it, so somebody broke the rules. And suddenly it didn't matter anymore whether it was solicited or not. So why should it matter at all?

Think about this for a moment. No Hogwarts ride at Universal Studios. No Butterbeer ice cream. No Voldemort

Halloween costume. All because of something as random and fleeting as the drifting gaze of a given literary agent. So, it begs the question why? Why did this agent do that on that day? Did they feel momentarily magnanimous after having a really good lunch? Was it an accident? Did her manuscript accidentally get mixed into the solicited pile? Did she believe in her dreams more than I did? These are questions I want answers to.

I'm getting pretty tired of the "she was a struggling writer but now she's a big success" narrative with all the important details edited out. So, now I'm writing about writing because for me, it has always run parallel to acting. I spent just as much time writing, copying, and mailing scripts as rehearsing for classes and showcases. I might have saved a whole lot in printing and postage if I had known more about how things really work. I applied to every writing fellowship, internship, and grant program I could find, one through the Motion Picture Academy (The Nicholl Fellowship), one for an actual position in story development at one of the studios.

Then, a funny thing happened on the way to the bathroom. I got a call from a writer friend who told me we had a job interview for staff writer positions on a children's TV show. What? Joe and I had co-written a teleplay the year before and apparently through sheer bluster, Joe had managed to hustle up a "pitch" session for both of us as a team. Great, I thought. We already are. So, we dressed up like first class shmucks and walked into a tall office building on Hollywood Boulevard ready to wing it out of the blue. Before hand, we had seen enough of the show to reference the characters and suggest storylines. Here's where improv training came in handy. Joe is also an actor, so that's what we did. We acted like we'd been doing this for years.

Each of us threw out plot ideas that seemed to go over really well with the two executives who interviewed us. We just went rat-a-tat-tat, pitching one after another. We even completed *each other's* ideas as we went along. The execs really seemed so jazzed by what we were coming up with, I saw them scribbling notes and when we finished, they both immediately smiled and stood up. "You guys are great! We think your stuff is fantastic! So, here's what we're going to do. We will call you next Tuesday and take it from there. We look forward to talking to you guys real soon. Thanks again." We all shook hands and left with a great feeling all around.

Next Tuesday came and went. Then, the Tuesday after that. Tuesdays have a way of doing that. If I'm really honest, I do remember that when he said, "we will call you next Tuesday," it sounded so cliché, there was a dismissive quality to it. I kind of knew they wouldn't let us wild men on their little show.

Several months later, one of the best story ideas we pitched that day sure enough appeared in an episode of the show. Of course, me telling you this is completely anecdotal hearsay. We have absolutely no way of ever proving what was said in that room and it's completely true that different writers can come up with the same idea. We were unknowns. We had signed nothing. They owed us nothing. Even so, the timing will always seem just a little too close for comfort. Seems like a good way of farming ideas without having to pay writers. Too bad you can't copyright what comes out of your mouth. You can however, things you write down, which is usually a good idea. It's easy these days with the Library of Congress website.

Allow me a moment to consider the actor *and* the writer together; if you are both, how do they relate to each other? For my own sanity, I've always tried to keep them in separate lanes because their workspaces are very different. And sometimes if you're not careful, they can interfere with each other. As mentioned, *too much* analysis and intellectualizing can undermine the looseness and freedom an actor needs to work. Conversely, too much looseness and improvisation can interfere with the discipline and eye for structure that a writer needs to maintain. So, in the prize-fight of the arts, I keep these two guys separated. They complement each other best when they are left to operate independently. *In the Birdcage* was a good example of a time when I found them working against each other. The actor couldn't fix what the writer had neglected because the writer was thinking too much about the actor. They kind of did each other in, so neither worked as well.

The best ideas for writing come directly from the deepest parts of you, the influences that move you, the things that affect you profoundly. It's hard to argue with honesty.

Expose yourself to books and movies that challenge your sensibilities, make you emotional, fearful, curious, inspired, or that make you laugh. If you dissect and study them very carefully, you will eventually discover what makes them work on you that way. The best art zeroes in on what is universal to the human experience. Find that in your own story idea and you might be on to something there. Really good writing, comedy or drama, is the science of communicating the most ideas with the very least number of words. So, I'll leave it with my favorite writing joke: a college professor of literature says to his class, "*Never* forget the importance of <u>brevity</u>. I once gave a three-hour lecture on it."

FACE IN THE CROWD

All right now, this is a difficult subject, so how do I put this delicately? Every day, busloads of people come to Hollywood without a notion of what is actually involved in pursuing a career. Kind of like me. Showbiz wraps itself in a shroud of mystery on purpose. It's part of the allure. Stardom is an invisible thing. There are so many apocryphal "making it big" stories, urban legends, and magical nonsense in the ether that feed people's curiosity. There's the famous story of Lana Turner being discovered on a stool in Schwab's ice cream parlor which, even if true is a one-in-a-zillion occurrence. It's no fun if showbiz, just like everything else, is really that arbitrary.

Also, thanks to the proliferation of reality shows like *American Idol*, many people have a completely distorted idea of what auditions are like and how decisions are made. No, *not* anyone can become a star. Also, a panel of judges doesn't watch you act for 30 seconds of Pinter and then tell you why you're great or you stink to your face. They wait until later and let your agent tell you. Also, giving away fame as a prize on a game show is not normal. In our fame-obsessed culture, it becomes understandable why show business attracts so many lost souls. There, I said it. A whole lot of wayward individuals who believe what they see on screen wander the streets of Hollywood—the derailed of the species, living on stories of romance and heroism on a grand scale that aren't real. If they only knew how much of what they see on the big screen is shot in big hollow barns with sawdust on the floor and power tools all over the place. It is this population that the industry must keep at bay so they can get a day's work done.

Two famous movie scenes come to mind. One from Bob Fosse's *All that Jazz*—in which Joe Gideon, the ladies-man choreographer (played by Roy Scheider) is trying to bed yet another little dancer. She innocently looks up at him and asks if he thinks she could be famous, "you know, like in the movies?" In spite of all the seductive lies he's told, he is forced to shake his head, no. The other is the finale of *The Day of the Locust*, where through the eyes of Todd Hackett, a brilliant young production designer, explosive visions of Hollywood burning to the ground fill his eyes as he is crushed by the rioting crowd at a world premiere movie. The novel by Nathaniel West also introduced the character of Harry Greener (played in the movie by Burgess Meredith) a washed-up ex-vaudevillian comic who, in his old age, is forced to scrape out a living selling miracle solvent door-to-door.

Fame, this thing everyone thinks they're after, is an amorphous commodity, a strange, random biproduct of an industry that de facto involves people watching you. Some have used it to manipulate people, some advance a social cause. Of course, most actors are *never* famous. Same with most musicians and artists.

Meanwhile, at the center of the hurricane, you have someone like John Lennon, who experienced an intensely exaggerated version of fame, admitting to feelings of imprisonment and extreme depression at the very height of his success, while the rest of the world watched in envy. It can be a scary, lonely place. And it rarely lasts. Or it can come and go multiple times and then evaporate. I think of my friend Darrel. It's not even really about you, per se. It's made of other factors.

I was once in a bar with a friend who introduced me to his good friend, an actress who had been a major Hollywood starlet in the 1970's, playing the sexy ingénue on a major primetime network show. I never would have known it was her if my friend hadn't told me. She looked old and tired with a leathery complexion, sitting quietly at the end of the bar. She told me she had barely worked since the show went off the air forty plus years ago. She reminded me of Jeff Porter, another guy I once watched holding court in a bar. He had starred in the number one TV show in America for four years and eventually drank himself to death.

This intense, unearned attention and/or the sudden loss of it has wreaked havoc on quite a few lives, usually those who are not prepared for the destructive fallout that can come with it. It can skew your entire view of life. There's nothing wrong with aiming high, but if fame by itself is the *only* goal, there are plenty of famous dead people—Marilyn Monroe, Janice Joplin, Lenny Bruce, Spaulding Gray, Michael Jackson, River Phoenix, John Belushi, Heath

Ledger, Phillip Seymour Hoffman. Even drug abuse and death get romanticized in media.

Also, if you do it early, dying can be the thing you become *most* famous for. And in our perverse pop culture, even that gets exploited by tabloids: "Inside—actual autopsy photos!" Nothing escapes the leering eyes of a star hungry mob. My hunch is it would be best to keep your priorities straight and not take yourself too seriously. Acting is something worth living for, not dying for. No gigs in the afterlife.

So, here you are. You may have studied and worked your whole life honing your crafts. You may be a responsible professional. Maybe even talented. This is the nut of the problem right here. The fact that the industry has no way of knowing *you* didn't just get off that bus, that you're not "The Guy" or some schlub waving his hand for attention, another face in that mob getting trampled in *Day of the Locust*. The ability to do this, to differentiate and get your talent noticed is both the most essential *and* the most difficult part of pursuing a career. How do you do that? Hell, I don't know. I'm the wrong guy to answer that one. Call George Clooney. Sorry I don't have more. I didn't mean to leave you hanging there. At some point, I stopped racking my brains about it. Better to accept reality, but still keep yourself open for a fluke, because that's actually what you need. And you're in good company. There's a lot of us out here.

THEATRE

Right now, in every major city, in every single state, there's a theatre director—a guru-like figure with a band of acolytes all around him who think he's God or certainly imbued with a superior creative knowledge. He sleeps with all his leading ladies (or men) and the guys all look up to him, largely for doing just that. It's a cultish, mini-David Koresh situation that pops up all over the place in college, community, and semi-professional theatre. He's in your town today, isn't he? If you sleep with the master, you will be a star and imbued with his special knowledge. Of course, it has nothing to do with making great theatre. It's more like an ego-driven power play that certain small-time operators take advantage of because they can. And they die one day like everyone else. That's when his followers find out he wasn't God after all.

So, if you can avoid the Koresh Playhouse, you might have yourself a rewarding theatre career. Regional theatre is a great place to get your land legs as an actor. People in regional theatre do it for any number of reasons. Not everyone has their eye on a professional career. Some do it as a hobby or a social occasion. That can result in some uneven shows, but by the same token, there have been many remarkably professional regional productions that miraculously click with the right confluence of cast, script, and director. They achieve an element of truth that connects with an audience.

An excellent live theatre production can be a remarkable experience you never forget, both for the audience and the performers. Like live music, it only exists in the now. Every performance is a unique event. I've been lucky in that most of my theatre experiences have been fantastically positive, challenging, and rewarding. A few duds of course, but that comes in the box. The great thing about theatre is the sense of creative community that can only come from a team of artists melding their talents live, in unison, like playing in a band. It's an exciting thing to be part of. And the right company can provide an ideal environment for an actor to build experience, discipline, and a real approach to the craft.

Oh, there is one more thing about being in a play. Just a minor pet peeve I'm hoping you can help me with. It's a phenomenon I've identified that I call "drift." This usually happens after a show has opened and the actors are settling into the rhythm of the scenes. A few shows into the run, they've had a chance to see which lines get the biggest audience reaction so the cast will begin to punch up certain lines, play down others, or get so loose with the dialogue that they end up paraphrasing or even adding lines they think are better. Hence, the show itself begins to *drift.*

A lot of actors think because they're onstage getting all the attention, their whims and notions are more brilliant than the writer. Here's where I always felt the need to pipe up on the playwright's behalf by mentioning that Neil Simon is gone and he's not here to object. Plus, he already did the hard part by giving us a great script, so how's about we honor his contribution by sticking to it?

The best directors I've worked with have a natural instinct to maintain a good grip on a show well after opening night in order to keep drift to a minimum. Lazy directors and actors do not, and the show can slip and slide all over the place. Please see what you can do about this and get back to me. Thanks. That's your only assignment.

Here's a few more thoughts on theatre. Theatre thoughts. Say it five times fast.

Theatre requires a lot of physical movement. Professional Broadway theatre requires the stamina of an athlete. It is by far the most labor-intensive gig there is. Most productions do eight or nine performances a week. They must, in order to pay for themselves. Rehearsal periods involve weeks of intensive hard work. So be ready. Everyone wants to be on the great white way, but when your day comes, they will get their money's worth out of you. That's why it's the greatest gig in the world. Don't forget rule number one though. Have major fun. For hundreds of years of human history, theatre was the *only* acting career in existence. It still remains the true birthing ground of all dramatic performance. And even if you never get to Broadway, you can still create that kind of standard for yourself in whatever production you are part of.

John Wilkes Booth's older brother Edwin Booth was a revered star of the theatre in his day. He was a gifted Shakespearean actor who historians have called the greatest *Hamlet* of the 19th century. It's interesting to note that John Wilkes Booth spent his life overshadowed by his older brother's stature and renown. That plus his confederate sympathies were a lethal cocktail of resentments that led up to his assassination plot. Being a theatrical guy, his grand plan was to shoot the president, leap onto the stage and yell, "Sic semper tyrannis! (thus always to tyrants!) The south is avenged!" thereby making his glorious last stand for the confederacy. However, he barely got out, "Sic sem . . ." when his foot caught in the flag bunting beneath the president's box and he fell to the stage, breaking his left leg. It always fascinated me that this actor with a bruised ego screwed up his one great, epic moment of onstage glory and ran limping out of the theater. Finally, after 12 days on the run, he died in a barrage of gunfire inside a burning barn. For the record, this is not a good theatrical career plan. As frustrating as it might get, there are better ways of going about it.

COACHING

I've always used the term "coach" to refer to people who have helped me develop as an actor, I suppose because acting is so physical and requires so much mental energy that every rehearsal feels like a workout. Or it should. Coaching is an art form unto itself. It requires infinite patience, infinite attention, and total acceptance of a person. Traits I don't possess but need very much from an instructor. I'm an actor who likes to be directed. I run fine on instinct, but it can be more exciting and challenging to deliver what an individual director wants. It makes you feel useful.

From the youngest age, I saw myself as a character actor and naturally was drawn to those kinds of actors on screen—Allen Garfield, Burgess Meredith, William Daniels, Ed Lauter, Anthony Zerbe, Ned Beatty. At the top of the list though, Gene Hackman's work occupied a massive space in my consciousness as a primary influence. There was something familiar there. His performances in *The Conversation* and *Scarecrow* have an honesty that for me transcend the camera and even the movie, cutting right through the screen to the head and heart. I wanted to know how to do that.

I also admired the work of John Cazale, who only made five movies and died of cancer at age 42. His short career represents some of the landmark film performances of his era—*The Godfather, Dog Day Afternoon, The Deer Hunter.* He was and is rightly regarded as an actor's actor. And yet, he didn't live long enough to experience a lot of his own success or receive the accolades he deserved. Shades of our artist friend Vincent. I wonder which is better, being regarded as a failure all your life and then a genius posthumously or to achieve a measure of success in life only to have it cut short?

These are the things I pondered on my jobs. So, imagine my delight when on a delivery run, in a high-rise elevator, Allen Garfield stepped in. "Excuse me, your name is Allen?" "Yes," he said. "Garfield?" "Yes." "Great to meet you. I'm an actor and a big fan." "Thank you," he said. I Introduced myself and after a brief actors' conversation on the long way down, he asked if I would like to join his scene study class. I didn't need to think too hard about that one. A chance to study with one of my influences. On the way out of the building, he gave me his home phone number and told me to call him.

By the following week, I was in his class, busy at work on a scene from *Glengarry, Glen Ross* by David Mamet. Allen paired me up with Zach who was an excellent scene partner. I was playing Richard Roma, a fast-talking real estate salesman opposite Zach as James Link, his hapless would-be customer. In the scene, Roma plies Link with alcohol and enough lofty rhetoric to get him to sign a contract for a swath of land in Florida, which he does and later regrets.

It's a terrific monologue with nice juicy subtext to play around with. Mamet's dialogue is notoriously choppy, abbreviated, and naturalistic, with a lot of crosstalk, interruptions, and staccato rhythms. Hard lines to memorize. Like Shakespeare, it requires a clear understanding of the vernacular and the overall story arc to guide you through.

I'll admit there were some moments in Garfield's class, watching him helping a struggling actor along that could be truly agonizing to sit through. Like a music student just picking up an instrument, you're going to hit a lot of wrong notes. But his patience and love for the work never let him give up on an actor. He also instinctively knew how to get the best out of each one individually.

I will never forget something he did for me during rehearsals of the *Glengarry* scene. We were doing a run-through. Toward the end of the scene, Roma picks up his briefcase, takes out a map of the Florida tracts, and unfolds it on the table in front of Link. Allen had seen us run it a few times. After we started, behind me and out of my view, he quietly moved my briefcase from where I had placed it, on the floor to my left, over to my right. When the beat came where Roma reaches for his briefcase, I was momentarily disoriented when I leaned down, looked both ways, and found it on the other side. But I immediately noticed how the interruption gave me a moment of unplanned spontaneity that lent a level of reality and a laugh too.

Through that simple gesture, Allen communicated so much. First, he was telling me not to get too comfortable. He wanted to shake me out of any pre-set behaviors that can stilt a performance. He was also showing me how to keep every beat fresh and spontaneous by staying out of one's safe place. He told me all that without having to say a word. I was honored he would trust me that way and I noticed it helped free up and flesh out *other* moments as well. He knew exactly what was needed and how to point me in the right direction.

Probably the single best, most salient actor's operating tool I ever learned from any coach comes in the form of a single question: <u>what do you want?</u> That's it. A simple but infinitely useful idea. What do you *want?* Think about your actual life. In an average day, inside your mind, you have wants every single moment of the day, major and minor. "I want to get up. I want to sit down. I'm hungry. I want food. I want to scratch my left arm." Even doing nothing is a choice and a want. Then, expand this to the next level. "I want to make someone jealous. I want to quit my job. I want that girl in the shoe store. I want people to believe _____about me." Sometimes you'll hear this idea referred to as "intentionality," a term I feel cheapens the concept which is much simpler. As we all know, wants can sometimes lead to *un*intended consequences. That's the fun part. After reading the script and character you are playing, it can be helpful to create a little yellow brick road of your character's wants through the story. Or not. If you can keep them clear in your mind every moment on stage, it's a handy inner roadmap. You can relax and just let the dialogue happen.

So, good coaching is about helping an actor's thought processes, which is why working with a good coach can be so enriching and exciting. I wish I could also tell you it's the key to a big, fat career as well, but I can't. It certainly helps if you're good, but it's not a requirement. Put on the TV right now and you'll see what I mean. Forever elevating your craft is an individual actor's task. Becoming a better actor is a lifelong project with or without a check stub attached.

A few years after I spent that entire summer beating the *Glengarry* scene to death, the movie version was released. I sat there watching Al Pacino play Roma and deliver that monologue so mellifluously, so superbly I was stunned. I knew every word and yet he made it feel fresh and effortless. Pacino's instrument is so finely tuned, he put that damn monologue over with a smoothness and mastery of Mamet's timing that was astonishing. Watching that movie was my final lesson on how to do that scene. Thanks, Al. Not much more to say.

While I was studying in Garfield's class, a working friend was cast in a movie with Gene Hackman. Holy smoke. Oh, my God. A chance to meet my inspiration. You mean I get to go straight to the top? I practically ran down to the set and spotted him over by the lunch truck. With my heart in my throat, I strolled right up to him. "Gene, my name is Dave Hern, and you are one of the reasons I'm an actor." He placed his hand on his chest and turned to me with an openness that surprised me. "Well, thank you very much, Dave." Within a minute or two, he turned the conversation to *my* career. "So, how is it going?" he asked. I laughed. "I'm working on it. Looking for an agent." He picked up my frustration. "People who come to town and start working right away don't appreciate what it takes to build a career," he said. "You have to hang in there. What do you want?" "Me?" I said. "I want to be working on this movie with you right now." "Really?" he said. "Because if that's what you *really* want, then I'll see you one of these days."

Getting a pep talk from my favorite actor was exactly what the doctor ordered. That was good enough to hold me for the next, oh ... rest of my life. Between Allen Garfield, Vincent Price, Al Pacino, and Gene Hackman, I'm grateful for some very good coaching.

NAKED AMBITION

One afternoon, I answered the phone and had to strain to hear an oddly quiet voice—a casting person who was calling directly in response to an audition I had completely forgotten about. It was for an episode of the *Playboy Video Magazine* on the Playboy Channel. They had been producing mini movies that were soft-core sendups of popular studio features. That means with topless women and lots of sex jokes added. The big movie in theatres at the time was *Stakeout* with Richard Dreyfuss and Emilio Estevez, a buddy/cop movie about two investigators on the stakeout of a suspect's girlfriend. So, this was the same story transposed for nudie TV and my character was to be the "geeky" partner of the duo. Had I had any sense of propriety, I might have thought twice, but starving actors take what they can get. Here I was being given a part outright that worked almost a week and paid money. So, I held my head up high and went off to conquer the world of soft-core skin flicks.

When I read the script, I thought maybe in spite of the material, I could at least get some laughs out of it. I also thought if I could do a believable character, maybe it would be worth it. So, I approached it with a tablespoon of Uta Hagen and a dash of Groucho Marx, my apologies to both.

The first day I arrived on set, the director was yelling at one of the lighting crew about the placement of a scrim. I was soon to find out that yelling was about all this person did. "ALL RIGHT! FILMMAKING 1-0-1! A SCENE IS A . . . SERIES . . . OF . . . SHOTS!! GOT IT? JESUS CHRIST!!"

After a while of listening to him unload on everybody from the actors to the catering crew, I figured out it would probably be in my best interest to just avoid the guy wherever possible, something I never imagined I could decide about a director. I was largely successful except of course for when we were rolling, then it was open season. "I SAID FASTER DOWN THE HALLWAY!! THAT GOES FOR ALL OF YOU!"

When I wasn't in a scene, I watched him working awhile from a distance. Here he was, this little Hitler guy letting all his frustrations out on his cast and crew. People with a lack of capacity for language tend to blame their inability to communicate on everyone around them. It was clear he saw himself as a genius auteur/wunderkind who's just too brilliant for these petty underlings to understand. As if this trash was the re-make of *Citizen Kane.* Well, I guess theirs would be *Tittyzen Kane.*

The first day of shooting took place in a municipal office building that doubled for the "Police Station" scenes. The guy who was playing my partner was a stand-up comedian who had worked the local clubs. He wasn't really an actor so much as a strong contender for "The Guy"— loud, can't relax, must be funny every second. So off camera, we didn't have much to talk about. He had one tic that threw me a little. He thought it was endlessly funny to suddenly blurt out, "He's got a GUN!!" To be fair, this was before the era of mass shootings but even so, is that a joke?

Now, since we were all working on a bunch of risqué sludge, it seemed to spur the alpha-male crew into a non-stop dirty joke-a-thon, each of them trying to out-filth each other. For pretty much the entire shoot, it was a cacophony of "ass-bump, titty-hump, bang the farmer's daughter, preacher's wife, Ben Dover, three-way, 69." Ok guys. I got it. They didn't even stop for lunch, keeping it going while you're trying to eat a meatball sandwich. Then, of course, back to the serious work.

One of the first things I had to do on set was get splattered with mud, since in the scene, my partner and I were supposedly tailing a notorious criminal into a mud wrestling club. After getting into costume, makeup, and mud, I felt like I was ready for anything. I was wrong. Two buxom women with lots of blonde hair showed up wearing bathrobes. They were guarded by two huge, muscular men who were either bodyguards or boyfriends or both. Then, as soon as we started rolling, the women threw off their robes and ran topless through the police station, making sure to bounce as much as possible for the cameras. Then, after the director yelled "cut," the muscle men covered them up again. It was interesting to observe the way they hovered nearby like male elephants guarding the herd. This went on all day until the girls ran out of bounce and the director ran out of insults for the day.

Day two was just as strange. Early in the morning, the entire cast and crew came knocking at the door of a huge mansion in Beverly Hills, supposedly the stakeout location. We were greeted at the door by the husband of the woman who was the featured player of the day. What that means is this friendly man was inviting an entire film crew into his home to film his wife naked. We all shook hands and the crew began moving all their gear inside. "Yes, hello, how do you do?" "This is my wife." "Nice to meet you." I'm thinking . . . yes, hello, this is my wife and these are her breasts. How are you all doing? We were invited into the kitchen for some refreshments. Then, they all went about the business of filming this woman stripping and flitting naked about her bedroom. I noticed that the director did not yell at her. It was clear this woman was a professional naked person.

However, the *real* professional arrived later in the afternoon. My leading lady, the actress who was to play the French maid, arrived and chatted with the director for a while, before coming over my way. I introduced myself. She had seemed pleasantly surprised by something he told her, so I asked her what it was. I learned she was a cross-over from hardcore pornography who had come fully prepared to perform explicit sex acts. The director had informed her she would not have to on this gig. Wasn't that great? Like I was supposed to share her relief and delight that she would not have to give me a blowjob. Whew! Yeah, lucky day huh? My fault for asking.

We plodded through our little scenes, and I picked up pretty quickly why her real job was not really "acting." She got the lines down but didn't seem to care at all what she was saying. When we got to work and I saw her up close, I thought she might have once been attractive, but now there was an angular asymmetry to her face and a tired look that she covered up with a lot of makeup. Also, her breasts were fake. Therefore, so was my "passion" for her in the scene. I thought, well I guess this is what I studied Stanislavski for. It felt like taking a deep breath, holding it, and diving under dark water.

Interestingly, the "climactic" part of the scene was filmed with me and everyone else out of the room altogether so that she would feel more comfortable faking orgasm. We all sat outside, quietly listening to three or four takes of her creaking the bedsprings, moaning, and groaning away. Shades of what might have been a beautiful romance. The director yelled "Cut!" and a strangely deep relief set in. That night I took a nice, long hot shower.

Post-production, it proved to be somewhat difficult to see the finished product. This was before cable was common and there were no DVRs. I didn't have the Playboy Channel and didn't know anyone who did. So, I hired a company that screens every channel and tapes whatever you need for your reel. They called me when the show was taped, so I went to their office where they let you view it in a private room. Thank God for that. I was pretty mortified. Whatever "character" I thought I was creating fell right through the sewer grate. Speaking purely objectively, I came off like a spastic jerk. I knew I could not even use it on my demo reel. All I was left with was a badly edited, incredibly unfunny piece of useless tape. To this day, I don't list the credit and only a few close friends have seen it because it's too goddam embarrassing.

So, let's just pretend I didn't even write this chapter and move on to the next one. Ok?

MORE JOBS

Yes. More jobs! Handfuls of them. Each time I got hired, I would sit down with yet another HR manager who would outline the company policies and suite of benefits as I would go numb in the head, knowing full well that I wouldn't be there long enough for any of it to matter. Certainly not long enough to hit any of their in-house "performance targets" or to qualify for Employee of the Quarter. I needed to keep a paycheck coming. That was my target. I was a seagull perched briefly on their 38th floor balcony.

At one point, sick of office buildings, I aimed for day jobs tangentially related to the industry where I thought I could work my way up. This happened fairly quickly, and I ended up on the lot of a major animation studio as a clerk in the computer tape library. This was when computer systems were in massive mainframe cabinets contained in huge, air-conditioned rooms, and data were contained in a massive library of tapes with coding on them that were in constant motion between users. It's funny to realize the entire contents of that library could now fit on a single iPhone, but was then state-of-the-art.

Of course, for me the fun part was getting to wander around the lot and see how things functioned. One lunch break at the cafeteria, I made a friend in Jason, one of the animators currently working on the studio's very first live action/animation hybrid feature. Once he realized he had a friend, over the next few months I got a detailed inside breakdown of the work that was going on. I threw him a million technical questions and learned about the processes used to overlay animated images onto live action footage. He broke down how dialogue was timed and other juicy tidbits. It was exciting to learn so much about the movie as it was being made. Oh, how I wished I was working on his side of the lot, but our conversations allowed me to enjoy it vicariously. My job tasks were at a point where it was doable on autopilot so I could spend more time trying to figure another way into a long-term job on the lot. After about nine months, it came time for management to make cuts. I was employed through a temp agency, so my animation studio days came immediately to an end. That's how it goes when you're a temp. The movie they were making went on to become a tremendous hit. I still think of that time whenever it airs on TV, as if I had anything to do with it.

Next, an ad caught my eye for what appeared to be quite a job—personal assistant to Howard H. Melnick, one of the biggest independent producers in Hollywood. I had an interview for the job in a small, plush office in Beverly Hills that smelled very clean. A short woman in a crisp business suit sat me down and took my resume. She spoke in a high, sing-songy voice. "Mr. Melnick gets his trades by 7:30 before breakfast. Mr. Melnick gets his dry cleaning delivered at 8:00. Mr. Melnick needs to arrive at the office by 9:00." Her voice had such a tinny rhythm, it was hard not to grin. The job was essentially this man's personal valet. How bizarre it seemed that a man could create a completely insulated life where every minor need or want is met by paid work horses. All because you're a movie producer? I kept thinking "when does Mr. Melnick get his ass wiped? Does Mr. Melnick eat with a bib?" I had an image in my head of Mr. Melnick vacuum-sealed in plastic, along with his dry cleaning. It wasn't me, but I'm sure they found the appropriate manservant for the job. All these years later, I wonder now that Mr. Melnick is dead, in the afterlife, does he still get his trades by 7:30?

Something similar happened at Tri-Star Pictures, where I had a job interview for a screening coordinator. Sounded like something I could do. Being a guy with a filmmaker's orientation, I thought I could bring something to it. Much to my dismay, this was in the executive offices where everyone wore a business suit. I was interviewed by two executives who I tried my best to warm up to, but it became clear this was the profit and investment arm of the company, not in any way connected to the film production side. It was kind of strange to hear the way they discussed movies as pure product and nothing else. Their literature consisted of earnings tallies for the month, quarter, and year. Fine, I thought. No auteurs here. Well, maybe I can just screen movies and forget the rest. I pretended I was eager for the job but was curiously relieved when I wasn't hired. I don't think I could have kept up the façade. The place was just too dry.

One night, trying to figure out the next move, it occurred to me that my experience as a corporate trainer of quality sons of bitches might help in the area of education. I saw an announcement that the Los Angeles Unified School District was having a teacher shortage and was issuing provisional credentials. It said there were substitute positions available that could lead to full time assignments. I went to the district office to apply and zipped through the process. Within a week, I was substituting. Then, I got a call from HR offering me a slot to complete a semester of middle school for a teacher who had left the term early.

So, almost right out of the gate, I had a full day of three periods to run—two levels of English and one drama class. I had to muster enough moxie to come up with enough material for six weeks of classes. My predecessor left nothing to indicate where each class was in any curriculum, what books were needed, etc. Neither it seems did the school's administration. But that was fine with me because I knew that's why they hired me. To figure it out. I did consider it a worthy challenge, but from the minute I entered the first empty classroom, I knew I had made a mistake. I felt clobbered with a heavy, disorienting sense of déjà vu. There was something creepy about suddenly being back in a dull green municipal city school building. Same blackboards and chalk, same alphabet and safety posters on the wall. The exact kind of classroom I was more than happy to leave behind as a student only about a decade earlier, except now I was the teacher. It felt cockeyed. But I resolved to see my commitment through.

Well, the drama part was relatively easy. I just recalled some of the actor's exercises I had been through over the years and presented them as something new. As a test of pure acting, one of my favorites involves putting a bunch of little slips of paper into a hat that everyone draws from. Each slip has one descriptive word written on it—Stunned, Drunk, Happy, Frustrated, Amorous, Frightened, Goofy, Confused, Nauseous, Melancholy.

Then, using only a dictionary for text, each student has to read aloud any random page while acting out the word they picked. The game is that the audience has to guess what the word is. The students got excited about this which was gratifying. Everyone got a lot of laughs too. Score another one for theatre.

The English was more daunting. I tried to assess where each class was in their reading levels and took it from there. The younger group needed basics like the parts of speech, the elements of a sentence, and a whole lot of writing time. The older kids I guess had either given up or stopped caring. I tried to give them some information about stories and writing, but I had more receptive audiences at my magic shows. So, I mostly let them read for the period which seemed more productive than arguing with them. I was glad they were reading at all.

By the fourth week, I started to feel like a fraud. I started watching the standard issue school clock on the wall, exactly as I had done all those years as a kid, waiting to go out and play. If you're going to be a teacher, be a good and dedicated one because that's what students deserve. I let my provisional credential expire shortly afterward largely because I didn't feel like returning to college and taking the swath of education courses required to keep it active. And besides, I knew inside I wasn't really a teacher. Don't tell any of my students, ok? If you're really an actor, the best they're going to get out of you is a good performance.

SOCIALLY DISTANT

I had a million acquaintances in the industry and a group I tended to hang with, but I didn't really have close friends in Hollywood. People you think you know do strange things. One night Peter, an actor friend, called me up rather late.

> "Dave, your roommate Bruce is diabetic, right?"
> "Yeah," I said.
> "You think you could you sell me some of his needles?"
> "I can't do that, Peter. I couldn't ask him for that."
> "Why not?"
> "He needs those for his health."
> "Well, you don't have to *tell* him. Couldn't you just *steal* some?"
> "Peter, are you serious? You want me to steal Bruce's needles so you can get high? I'm not doing that. What I'm doing is going back to sleep."

With junkies like that, who needs friends? You may be saying come on now, Dave. Where's all the raunchy stories about your wild times with all those Hollywood girls? Well, I sure wish I could report some of that, but the truth is with women in Hollywood, every relationship had quotes around it and lasted as long as an episodic TV gig.

Two come to mind. At a party one night, I met a beautiful dark-haired woman who didn't talk about herself much, but seemed impressed that I was in an episode of a TV show that week. It was just a coincidence, but it didn't hurt to have something to show for myself. A few days later, after the show aired, she called me up and invited me over. Her place was covered with posters of Marilyn Monroe who she talked about a lot to the point where I began to wonder what kind of worship society was happening there, but I let it go of course because I was in a cute girl's place. Anyway, we pretended we had a relationship going on for a few weeks, until she soon realized that I wasn't on TV *every* week. She couldn't say any of it out loud, but her disappointment that I wasn't a TV star became obvious. Finally, one night she ranted, apropos of nothing, "I deserve nice things and don't want to have to work hard all my life to get them!" Well, I'm sorry I was not able to provide her a bonified high-end life with a pre-certified rich and famous actor, so we let our blossoming simulated romance die a quick, well-deserved death.

While paying the check at a diner one morning, I noticed a lovely young blonde woman sitting at the counter looking rather down. She was sniffling and I thought she might be crying so I asked if she was ok. She smiled and thanked me and said she was just getting over a cold. I ended up walking her out and up the block chatting with her and she seemed quite bright.

I offered her a ride which she accepted. "We better get you something for that," I said and pulled into a Walgreen's parking lot to get her some antihistamine pills. She gobbled a few and quickly started feeling and looking much better.

She really seemed quite pleasant and upbeat for the rest of the day and we talked for hours. At one point, she was overcome with sadness, and I asked her what was wrong. "Oh," she said shaking her head. "You're a *really* nice guy." "So?" I asked. "Isn't that good?" Later that night, I drove her home to my apartment and cooked her some dinner. We listened to music until I started to nod off and told her she was welcome to the sofa if she liked and I was going to sleep. Without any hesitation, she followed me into the bedroom and jumped into bed with me in about a minute. Certainly not unwelcome.

Much later, after I had fallen asleep, I awoke to the sound of my front door rattling. I got up and found her dressed, pulling on the front door handle which was stuck. "I thought you were staying," I said. "I gotta get back," she said, so I yanked the tricky doorknob and let her out. "Good night," I said and she scampered away into the darkness. About a millisecond after I closed the door, I noticed my wallet on the desk and scooped it up to find that, yes indeed, she had stolen my money. She didn't take the credit cards, just the cash which might have been fifty bucks. Damn. I let her out with my money. Had I waited one more moment, I might have caught her. Sad part is, I probably would have just given it to her if she needed it. Then I realized why she had looked so sad earlier. What she was really saying was, "I'm sad because you're a *really* nice guy and I'm going to rip you off." She was a street urchin. Never knew her name. Never saw her again. I did have other semi-girlfriends and somewhat relationships over my decade in Hollywood, but for some reason, those are the two that stand out as being the most representative of the emotional landscape I was living in. Pretty barren. I didn't fall in love or get married or have a family. It didn't even feel possible there. For the most part, I felt like I was wandering a wasteland.

Even when I had a girlfriend, things were too strange. My girlfriend Arlene's father used to flip houses, so she would occasionally housesit in various properties that were in probate or mid-flip. One night, she invited me over to a house she was occupying for a few days. She asked me to bring my guitar since her brother was visiting. He was learning guitar and bringing his, so she thought we could play together. I brought my steel string, and we did indeed jam for a while. The house was empty, so it had great acoustics. He showed me a few rock tunes he had been working on and I played some blues riffs. Altogether, we played a good hour until I needed a break and a cold drink.

When I headed down the hall to the back rooms, I noticed the walls were covered with a black, powdery dust that looked like it had been smeared there on purpose. "Hey, your cleaning crew missed the hallway!" I called. "Oh, the cops put that there!" she said. When I returned looking confused, she explained that there had been a double murder in the house and the forensics team had been dusting for fingerprints. I find this out after we had been merrily jamming the night away.

So, as a point of musical pride, I can now say that I once played the ballroom of the Oakland Claremont Hotel, where I played to a room of live people and once, the living room of a house in LA, where I played to a room of dead people. I hope we didn't violate some cosmic rule. Do you think maybe they got a little groove out of it?

PARTY DOWN

I can't count the number of times I was told I should go to a party because "_____ is going to be there." There are lots of parties in Hollywood. Parties at clubs and parties in bars and parties at people's houses. I knew a lot of comedians, so I went to parties at The Comedy Store, The Improv, and The Laugh Factory. To me, a party means a get together with some close friends to enjoy some food and good company. In Hollywood, it's an entire street level career activity that is exhausting and relentless. I met famous actors, singers, and porn stars at these parties. I admit I was never very good at the retail enterprise of schmoozing in the name of your career. I felt bewildered by the whole scene. I was out of place and no doubt it showed. I once went to a "Launch Party" for a TV show that never aired. And yet it was in a huge, packed club with celebrities attending. I was introduced to Mike Tyson that night. How he got there, I have no idea. People say things like, "Hey, it's all about who you know. If you ever want to work in this town, you don't want to miss this opportunity." Opportunity for what? To sit next to a famous person who you don't know eating oysters?

My friend Corey found success early and landed on a major Network TV action show that had already been a hit for several seasons: a shoot-em-up with stunts and explosives, car chases, etc. One afternoon, he invited me to visit him on location, so I went to his trailer where, between the times they needed him on set, we did a little work on a stage play we had been writing. I met the other "stars" of the show and munched some lunch while we worked. At one point, a pretty woman stuck her head in the trailer checking on Corey, who invited her in, which of course destroyed any further attempts to write. I tried, but you know how certain guys, when in the presence of a pretty woman, suddenly get stupid and lose all discipline and rationality? Corey drew her into our discussion of the play which she knew nothing about, but she tossed her head back and forth and chimed in a few suggestions Corey felt a sudden need to agree with. Uh-oh. I could see this was not going to be a productive dynamic, so I left and came back later after she was gone.

When I returned to the trailer, there was a small gaggle of people hanging around chatting with Corey. I guess you could call them location trolls, people who follow TV and movie sets around, trying to meet and be around celebrities and showbiz people. This was a tall guy with his arms around two women with short dresses. Corey clearly had his eye on one of the girls. A couple of other mutual friends had shown up as well. It was obviously now the dreaded "party time." I didn't have anywhere else to be, so I sort of rolled with it.

These people had a flat not far from the location so the whole bunch of us drifted over there. It was a walk-up with black painted interior and various neon sculptures on the walls and on a few free-standing pedestals. The place was already smokey as we entered, and my friend Larry and I eventually found a place to sit on a sofa. Someone passed around a joint which I puffed on.

Our hosts were a strange bunch and I kept trying to discern what the relationships were here. They all got drunker and stoned-er while kind of flirting with each other. Does this guy live with both these women? Is this a menage situation or am I just thinking creatively? And what are they after? My gut said something bad was here. Larry nudged my left arm. "Hey Dave, did you hit that doobie?" he asked. "Yeah," I said. "That one?" he asked. "Yeah," I said again. "Oh no," he said. "That one's dusted! They think it's funny." He was telling me I had just hit a joint laced with PCP, a drug I would never touch. "Listen to me," he continued. "Things are going to get really strange for a while."

I thank God Larry was there to warn me, because if he hadn't, I probably would have just figured I was losing my mind. I gradually began feeling very edgy and tight, the opposite of pleasure, an intensely negative, paranoid sensation of being dosed with heavy chemicals. It felt like I was grinding my teeth down to the nubs, sitting there rooted to the sofa—so heavy I could barely move. An odd metallic taste formed in my mouth, like I was sucking on a razor blade. I took an internal snapshot of this moment in my mind. So, this is Angel Dust. Why would anyone do this voluntarily? Don't people do drugs to feel *good*? This is horrible. I suddenly understood why people do insane things on it.

Then, in the midst of all this, I heard laughter. My hosts were enjoying the fact that they had dosed me. I could see them pointing at me and giggling with their faces stretching out, like in a funhouse mirror. Everything visual became more extreme. The neon appeared brighter, and I could feel no sense of time. I couldn't even tell how long we had been there, so I just hunkered down and tried to ride it out. I heard someone mention food at one point and before I could really get myself together, the whole crew was on the move again. I was still not in any kind of operable condition, so memory says Larry and others must have helped me along to the diner where we all ended up.

I had enough sense to know that getting some food in me would be a good idea. I have no memory of what I ate, but I was starving, and it did help me begin to normalize a little, which went against the grain of the group because by this point our hosts were getting drunker, louder, and crazier by the moment. Larry suggested we leave, but Corey was still busy focusing on the girl. The whole situation now felt dangerous. Before long, I heard a loud crash of breaking glass. The man had smashed a bottle and thrown his drink across the room. He was on his feet screaming at all of us and getting aggressive toward the girls. Then, before I even knew what was happening, we had all scattered in different directions like a bunch of cockroaches in the light. No goodnights, no see-you-laters.

In the night air, I found myself running blind as steadily as I could. I thought I heard a police siren off in the distance as I ran, filling my lungs with the cold night air, no idea where I was, coming down while trying to find my way home. Somehow, I did and felt so grateful when I could finally lay down. Later, after some quiet time, I wondered how an ordinary day that began with visiting a friend for some writing, ended in violence, paranoia, and panic? Is this how you party in Hollywood? I hope I've got this down now.

Every year at Christmas time, my acting crew and I would perform a silly little routine in which we get together for a holiday hobnob and sit around talking about the year that had been, the coming one, what we were looking forward to.

Inevitably, depending on how stoned everybody was, someone would say, "I think this is going to be the year"— meaning the year that we all hit big and become rich and famous actor guys.

Meaningless Statement Log:

A. "Everything is leading in the right direction, man."

B. "I mean, this is it! The wave is coming."

C. "No doubt, something's about to hit. And it's going to be huge."

D. "It's inevitable. We're too good."

E. "This year just *feels* different, you know?"

Then, the following year, we would get together and say, "No, **THIS** is the year it happens. Forget last year." God Bless the struggling actor. It's hard to be your own rooting section. Sometimes, this stuff can be very comforting when nothing else is. Why the hell not? Have some more eggnog. One more holiday shot of self-confidence never hurt anybody. Maybe Santa will leave you an agent under the tree.

EROSION

In Los Angeles, nearly everywhere you go, you can't escape the pervasiveness of Hollywood. Massive movie billboards all along Sunset Boulevard. Bronze stars on Hollywood Boulevard. The walls of nearly every barber shop, diner, deli, or garage are decorated with autographed pictures of celebrities: "Thanks Walt, for a super brake job. Love ya, Frank Sinatra." "Leanest pastrami in town, Hank. Love to the gang, Ed McMahon."

In the 1980's as I struggled away, my father made a small comeback in the industry, appearing in various TV gigs and as a semi-regular on *L.A. Law.* My coaches were established character actors, and my roommate was a page at CBS television city. I was fully immersed in a life where seeing my father, my friends, and my teachers on TV or movie screens was commonplace. Also, various auditions and interviews lead me onto every major studio lot, casting office, and into screening rooms at both SAG and the Directors Guild. So, even though I didn't really have a career, my proximity to everything in the industry sustained an *illusion* of involvement. Everything is close, but very far away. It can distort your perspective.

I used to imagine what I would say to Jimmy or Johnny or Oprah or whoever's show I was being interviewed on. But then I would kick myself and say, "Dave, they want to hear from *successful* actors, not ones nobody ever heard of." I do wish someone would've pulled my coat just once and said, "*Psst*! Dave, it's an inside job. Quit banging your head against the wall." If you are lucky enough to become a real working actor and/or writer, many of the obstacles and roadblocks I've discussed turn around and systems begin to work in your favor. A good agent gets you good jobs. Good jobs earn you great benefits through the union. Good stuff begets good stuff. Or as Ray Charles said, "them that's got are them that gets."

My decade in Hollywood began to slip when one Friday morning at work, I learned that three different opportunities I had been waiting to hear about for months all fell apart within a few hours of each other. I had applied for a writing fellowship with the Motion Picture Academy; I was up for a possible TV role; and a writing partner and I had submitted a script to Sundance Institute's development program. By that afternoon, they had all crashed and I went from being a guy with projects, plans, and irons in the fire to an office manager with a day job and nothing else. Somehow the trifecta of the three strikes felt profound—like a wall had collapsed behind me and I couldn't go back. I shed a tear in my business suit and had to duck into a bathroom to gather myself.

That incredibly hot weekend, I spent sweating and gasping away, pouring water on my head, trying to cool my body temperature down any way possible. I saw a cheap swamp cooler advertised in a newspaper flyer and hit the freeway to pick one up. I drove it home, set it up, and watched it stir the air a tiny bit without cooling anything. I threw it back in the car and was headed back to the store when the engine suddenly exploded with a loud *CLANG*. The car drifted to the side of the road in a plume of black smoke and died right then and there on the Hollywood freeway.

This was the green Pontiac that was the period to my sentence. I jumped out and stood there staring at it, reviewing the situation. Not knowing what to do, I sold it for scrap to a tow driver right off the median strip. Somehow, just the process of trying to cool off was more than the system could handle. Time seemed to stop and at that moment my entire Hollywood existence felt pretty silly and pointless.

My career collapsed and then the car blew up. I can take a hint. Time to go.

SECRET AGENTS

Even though I had decided to leave, I *still* took one more Hail Mary pass at representation, looking in vain for a last-minute excuse to stay. The agent hunt had been a never-ending enterprise. I would get a burst of energy and try again, taking stabs at it until it ran out. Eventually, out of desperation, I let two guys I barely knew or trusted function as my agent at different points. I needed so badly to approximate something that looked or felt like a career.

The first was Clarence, a rotund, genteel black gentleman with a pencil thin mustache who I met early in my LA journey. He wore satin smoking jackets and had a love of martinis. In fact, when I first met him, he was shaking one up on the backyard patio of his house, which also functioned as an outdoor office with a desk, phone, and open bar. Nice work set up he made for himself, but I rarely saw much else going on. He had valid business cards, and I did see him answer the phone a few times. But mostly, he'd come up with more occasions for a toast. He told me who he knew and what he wanted to do with the agency.

I liked Clarence. He was a jovial, genuinely sweet person, so it was hard to express anything negative or show any frustration at the fact that nothing at all was happening for months and years. I didn't mention him earlier because it never felt like he was actually there. He only appeared to be representing me theoretically. So, I went about my business thinking of him as a number to call if I nabbed any work on my own. Just like not having an agent at all. And that was the condition for my entire run there.

So now I'm on the phone again for one last lovely spring afternoon of hang ups and rejection, remembering—oh yes, this is why I stopped doing this last time. It's futile and draining. But then, a woman with a quiet older voice answered and when I asked if she would meet with me, rather sweetly replied, "Yes, of course" and gave me an appointment time the next day. Well, that gob-smacked me pretty good. After hanging up, I kept glancing at the address I scribbled just to make sure it was real.

Her office was in a tiny, cramped walk-up off Hollywood Boulevard. The walls of the agency were so tight I had to turn sideways to get into the office. Linda Burress, the owner sat at a wooden desk with cigarette burns on it and I could see what looked like smoke stains on the walls and ceiling, evidence of years of chain smoking. Her husband Roger appeared to be doing most of the agenting, bustling about amid papers and resumes which were piled up everywhere. As we talked, I noticed a large, signed photograph of Rudy Vallee on the wall behind her. Vallee was a crooner of the 1920-30's, famous for singing romantic love songs through a megaphone, which became his signature image. "Oh yes, Rudy was my client for years," she told me proudly. "I booked one of his last concerts."

Linda spoke to me as if I were an old friend who already knew a lot of what she was telling me. This certainly felt promising, and her stories were interesting. But I wondered if she was mistaking me for somebody else. When we were wrapping up, she matter-of-factly told me to "leave some pictures with Roger" and said they would be in touch soon.

A part of me knew she was quite possibly senile which may be why she invited me in the first place. She was too dizzy to remember to tell me to get lost. So, I didn't want to ask her directly if she was officially representing me or signing me or God knows what. I just thanked her and left. Fine. She likes me. That's enough. Let's see how it goes. After a few more weeks of nothing, I returned to the business of leaving—sorting through a decade's worth of bric-a-brac, which just like my life there, no longer had any real purpose. But it's hard to get out of LA. Something always seems to pull you back.

Like the last-minute surprise that was waiting . . .

HAPPY NIGHTMARE

I love everything about a set; the noise, the people scrambling back and forth, the miles of cable running everywhere and the general sense of controlled mayhem. It's exactly how I wanted to spend every day of my life. And the few times I've been lucky enough to work, I have savored like a melting nugget of smooth chocolate, going down ever so deliciously.

I was already halfway packed when the call came through that I had been waiting a decade for. A job. Through a casting director. An actual job in an actual TV show, the role of Dr. Rothman, a psychiatrist in an episode of *Freddy's Nightmares*—the syndicated TV version of the *Friday the 13th* movies. There it was. I couldn't believe my name was on a call sheet. I had a call time and a set to report to. Dearest Holy Mother of Showbiz, thank you for this blessing. Also, thanks to Jesus, Mohammed, and Vishnu.

The set was contained in a large, empty warehouse in Culver City that looked like it used to store appliances or auto parts. To me, it was heaven on earth. A place to do what I love. When I arrived in the morning, I was shown to my trailer. That's right—a trailer that had my name on it. Outside was a chair with my name on it as well. Everyone was so welcoming, it felt like I'd always worked there. The first assistant director said, "Oh, you got the famous trailer!" and explained that it had been used by Arnold Schwarzenegger and Liza Minelli. I remember looking at the toilet and pondering if we had all shared the throne. I was told that I could report to makeup whenever I was ready and that the breakfast buffet was open. What kind of life might I have led had this been my morning routine instead of waking up on a conference room floor?

After getting into costume and makeup, I helped myself to a plate of waffles and looked for a place to sit. I found an overstuffed chair sitting in a large chunk of set that looked like the corner piece of a living room, off by itself. As I ate, I caught a flashing glimpse of myself in an adjacent mirror. It felt like I was in some kind of Valhalla. In that moment, I felt the most complete sense of wholeness I think I've ever felt. Here I am, employed at my job, getting fed breakfast, in good company, enjoying being alive. It doesn't get much better. A tiny cry of joy escaped me between bites.

I was introduced to my co-star, Phil, who played Dr. Crowley, the chief hypnotherapist at Springfield Hospital. We clicked immediately which made the whole process a pleasure. It's fortunate when you get paired off with an actor you can fall into rhythm with. Our leading lady was an actress I had seen in a million commercials. And our director was a real pleasant and efficient guy in the way he dealt with the crew and actors. For each shot, we ran a quick camera rehearsal and knocked out a few takes. Everyone operated at about the same pace so each day wrapped on schedule. At lunch on the second day, I overheard Phil talking about the *Firesign Theatre*, a comedy group on record, that I had grown up listening to. I had many of their albums in my collection. Then I realized Phil was Phil Proctor of the *Firesign Theatre*. I had worked a whole day with him and hadn't put it together.

Then of course I let it all slip about the albums, my fandom, etc. What a thrill, to play opposite a guy I had always admired. It made the rest of the experience that much more exciting. I didn't want the shoot to end. When it did, it felt so anti-climactic. I thought, you mean I can't just come back tomorrow and continue? I would have been perfectly happy to return to that dusty barn and say that silly dialogue every day for the rest of my life. It was such a rich taste of the life I love; it made it even harder to go back to whatever day job I had at the time, which interestingly, I can't remember.

A couple of months later the episode aired at 2:00 in the morning when you're lucky if *anyone* is watching. And the series was cancelled shortly thereafter. And I still had no agent. None of that mattered. I had a wonderful time and enjoyed every minute. But when the job ended, so did any reason for staying. That was as far as I could get. There was nothing left on the horizon.

*The episode has since been sold in a season package to a platform for Amazon Video which means a whole new generation of viewers can now enjoy watching a copy machine operator playing a psychiatrist.

RETURN UNUSED PORTION

Here's some more stupid stuff I did. Fast forwarding a chunk to northern California about a year later, out of the blue comes a call from Roger with an audition. He mumbled, reading the details haltingly, even slower than Linda and a bit unsure of even who he was talking to or whether or not I was still in town. Despite my questions, I couldn't decipher if it was a movie or a TV show, but I did get the call time out of him and the address of the casting office. Fine. I figured it's better than no audition.

So, I booked a flight *back* to LA, a rental car, and got myself there on time. Feeling ready for action, I strolled into the office, found the sides, and immediately realized it was a cattle-call for background and bit actors for the re-enactments on a cheesy syndicated true crime show. These are no credit, almost no pay gigs. I was quickly lost in the shuffle and realized I had just wasted air fare, gas, and time. How embarrassing. Caught my plane back home and pretty much wrote the whole thing off.

A few months later comes a call from Jimmy, a guy with a sharp, confident disc jockey voice telling me that he's a friend of the Burress Agency and he had taken over the office, found my pix/res and liked my look. What happened to Roger and Linda? They had both passed away within a month of each other leaving the agency unattended. This really hit me. I remembered them both as nice people and it seemed so sad to know that I had been witness to the tail end of their lives and careers. Jimmy said he wanted to meet and represent me. Well, having never heard anything like this, it got my attention. On top of that, he told me he would cover my air fare and accommodations for the visit. I thought, well, this guy has the salesmanship part down. This was in the pre-zoom world, so I didn't know what he looked like, but the deal sounded pretty good. So, Dave the Moron gets on a plane _again_.

At the airport curb, Jimmy picked me up wearing a T-shirt and jeans, driving a fairly beat up station wagon convertible. He introduced me to a girl named Donna sitting in the passenger seat who looked slightly unkempt and was busy applying makeup. She said hello but didn't turn around as I got in the back seat. "Where do you want to go now, baby?" he asked her, driving slowly around the pickup circle. "Weren't we going to your office?" I asked. "Sure," he said and off we went. Jimmy filled the drive time with anecdotes about the industry people he knew including Walter, an executive producer on The West Wing who he said he would be introducing me to.

I expected to arrive at the same location where I had met Linda and Roger, but instead we pulled up to the front of an older marble-lobbied building and went upstairs to what was an even smaller office space, still largely in disarray from either a move in or out. We sat around chatting while I waited for him to mention anything about what I was there for. He liked to compliment Donna on her looks because she liked hearing it, so I sat watching them do that for a while.

I tried a few times to nudge the conversation in a business direction, but each time I brought it up, he said, "We'll talk about all that tomorrow." Later, as we left the building, Donna said goodbye and went her own way. Jimmy then drove me to the "accommodations" which turned out to be his apartment in West LA, a unit in one of the myriad pre-fab stucco complexes with a small pool surrounded by identical walk-up units and a bank of mailboxes in the lobby. We were greeted by Jimmy's wife, which surprised me since that's what I thought Donna was. Jimmy could see a little confusion on my face, so when she went to the bathroom he explained, "I have a purely business relationship with my wife." That sounded even stranger, but I figured this guy wants to represent me, roll with it. Jimmy told me I could sleep on the sofa. The next morning, he cooked up a huge bacon and egg breakfast which I appreciated as I was ravenous. I thought I was there to get signed by an agent. I never expected to be drawn so directly into this guy's personal life.

We hit the road for the NBC studios where he whispered something to the man in the guard booth and we were issued onto the lot. Jimmy led me to the *West Wing* set where we found Martin Sheen in a T-shirt and shorts working on his lines in his trailer. "Hey Marty!" Jimmy called and introduced me. "This is Dave, one of my clients."

"Nice to meet you," Martin said. "Are you working the show today?" Surprised and delighted, I blurted out, "Whew, I wish!"

He went back to work and for the next hour or so, I walked around pondering how great life could be reporting there for work every day. Jimmy schmoozed everyone he ran into until he eventually found Walter, who he spent quite a while chatting up. Walter looked distracted, like he was trying to disengage, but Jimmy kept going until Walter interrupted him and excused himself to go back to the set. "Great guy," Jimmy said. No introduction. No mention of it either.

As the time passed, it became obvious that Jimmy had no leverage at all. He just wanted to impress me with the fact that he could get access to the NBC lot and the *West Wing* set but had no real plan to get me on the show. Did he seriously think he could hustle a role into existence? Where's the casting director? I reluctantly realized that Jimmy was just a top shelf bullshit artist, a studio pest. I mean, so far, he had lied about his office, his wife, my accommodations, meeting Walter, and what we were doing on the lot. I even started to wonder if Roger and Linda had really died. I wanted to go home and look for a real agent. After Jimmy ran out of people to hustle, we headed back to Jimmy's apartment as I checked my watch for the time until my return flight.

Jimmy put on the TV in the middle of a documentary about the civil rights struggle of the 1960's. It had a lot of interesting footage I had never seen before of Malcolm X and other movement leaders of the time. Jimmy shook his head. "You know, killing Martin Luther King was probably the smartest thing they could have done. I mean, he was getting the blacks all riled up, you know?" Oh my god, I thought. I am in the care and feeding of a *racist*, sleazy, lying scumbag. At that moment, I didn't know whether to scream, vomit, punch him in the face, or all three at the same time.

Instead, like a coward, I swallowed my cud and stayed mostly silent for the remaining hours until he could get me back to the airport. To this day, I feel shame for that. It was one of those moments of blunt force truth that test your ethical limits. And I failed. I compromised myself more than I ever imagined I could. All because I needed a goddam agent. Even worse, I gave him one more chance a few months later when he called and wanted to visit me in Oakland. I can't believe I let Hollywood nonsense drag me so far down to a place I couldn't tolerate or justify living in. So, I dumped Jimmy after calling him every name in the book. But, at that moment, I probably deserved a few myself. The whole damn episode shut the lid on looking for a Hollywood agent. I felt like a shmuck the size of a balloon in the Macy's Thanksgiving Day Parade.

Rule #2-F. Never get on a plane without at least a speck of peripheral knowledge of where the hell you are going and why.

EXODUS (Movement of Jah Person)

Going back was a mistake. Why didn't I heed the fact that originally, almost from the second I had decided to leave, my luck began to turn? I held a sidewalk rummage sale of my crummy furniture and sold every piece the first day. Someone bought a guitar off me. My tax refund miraculously showed up. I found ten dollars in the zipper pouch of an old suitcase. Cash was what I needed to get out, so in an extremely sad episode, I sold off my suitcase of magic equipment—the last of my toys really, along with the red velvet-lined magician's podium that my father had custom made for me. I wrestled mightily with this. They had been sitting in the closet for my entire LA life and the skills were rusty. Magic is to be shared and enjoyed, so in the end I sold it all for $200 to a friend with kids who I knew would enjoy it. Probably also destroy half of it, but what the hell.

I went through the mental checklist of things to give "one more chance" before I ran away. Clarence was one of them. I secretly wished he had some miraculous new plan or some fantasy role he had been hiding in his desk. "Oh Dave, please don't go! You're my most important client!" I imagined him saying. "We're just getting started!" But I couldn't convince myself anymore, so I decided to just ask him point blank if there was any reason for me to stay. I found him exactly as I had left him, shaking up a martini. He looked as dapper and jolly as ever and a bit surprised to see me. I never wanted to disrupt his cocktail party, but this time my world was crumbling.

"Clarence, I need to get dead serious with you for a second, my friend. Is that ok?" I asked. He looked at me and put the shaker down. We then sat and had probably the best conversation we ever had. He was honest and confessed that he couldn't really give me what I wanted to hear but wished he could. "I'm just not able to at this point, Dave. You need high-level rep. But I really do hope for the best for you." I finally joined him in a toast to my departure.

I finished packing, rented a U-Haul truck, and loaded up the remnants of my material life. I quickly realized what a paranoid existence I had been living because after hitting the road, I didn't feel safe until I was out of LA county. I kept thinking either the cops or some county official was going to drag me back to pay some overdue fine. But I made it to Oakland without incident.

IN THE END

One morning in my late forties, I woke up and realized that an entire generation of actors had been born, grew up, secured representation, and commenced full-blown careers all just in the time I'd been looking for an agent. Wow. How did that happen? Hollywood has a way of draining years off your life and you don't even notice. In my case, a decade. It was sobering to realize I can't play young men anymore. Gone are the twenty- and thirty-somethings and they're never coming back. I can't go back now and will myself a long and storied career. It didn't happen that way.

I have a nightmare that unfolds like the end of Dickens' *A Christmas Carol* where I'm suddenly in a dark, windy graveyard approaching my own headstone, but instead of my name engraved there are instead the grand totals of all the copies, faxes, and pieces of mail I delivered in my life.

- When I die, there will be no mention on *Entertainment Tonight* about my passing.

- There will not be a montage of shots from my films at the Oscars "In Memoriam" segment.

- It will not appear on Google, Yahoo, or other search engine face pages.

- Ironically, my name _will_ finally appear in SAG-AFTRA magazine.

But don't cry for me, Argentina. My story has a happy ending. There are different ways to total it all up. When it comes to the fungible, it isn't even close. I'm completely in the red. Over a lifetime, I have easily spent five or more times the amount of money on the career as I have ever earned back as an actor. That's what acting is—something you pay for until one day they decide to pay you for it. Or not. I was lucky enough to enjoy a few brief stretches of survival but nothing you could ever call a living. Did I make mistakes? Of course. I behaved clumsily all over the place. No doubt I blew opportunities. I said the wrong things to the wrong people at the wrong times. Even so, I think the average jury would acquit me.

As far as writing goes, do you know how some people have their finger on the pulse of public taste, just an instinctive sense of what will excite a large number of viewers? You know that guy? Ok, I'm the _opposite_ of that guy. I have no comprehension whatever about how the American consumer of entertainment thinks. I'm completely mystified about why certain things are tremendous hits and others tank. My whole orientation is not on that track. The whole time I lived there, deep inside was the growing realization that I just don't _think_ like Hollywood and never really did. The art that I had to sell, Hollywood was not interested in.

But then there's the intangible—the miraculous and the magical. I once had an audition on the 20th Century Fox Studios lot. I purposely arrived early so I could use my day pass to check everything out. Movie lots are some of the coolest places on earth. They have a cafeteria; some have a little museum of their Oscars and other memorabilia. Plus, there are the big steel hangars that hold the studios themselves. As I rounded a corner, I wandered to a place where I found myself alone in that part of the lot.

I came upon a full-sized outdoor re-creation of a New York City neighborhood, circa 1950, complete with fake walk-down subway stations, streetlamps, and store fronts. Without a beat, I launched into my own little "Singin' in the Rain" dance down the street, swinging around the lamp posts, except I think I was singing "New York, New York." I truly love moments like that. They fill me with delight. They remind me of why I built a life around this stuff. They're just simple, joyful moments you are free to enjoy, and no one can ruin them.

So, in spite of all the commercialism of Hollywood and after all the rejection, the one thing they can never corrupt is an actor's pure love for the work. You know the famous emblem of theatre, the two masks—one smiling, one sad, representing comedy and tragedy? I always loved the simplicity of that and how much it represents about us. We're happy and we're sad. That's what art is for—to reflect our joy and heartache and every emotion in between.

The love of acting makes you want to leave something simple and true like that behind, some small symbol or touchstone that tips a hat to the complexity of human beings at their deepest level, something to evoke the highest moments art can bring—a poetic sonnet, a magnificent preacher's sermon echoing through a cathedral, a dancer's impeccable pirouette, a conductor's symphonic crescendo, a cry of players. Or a primal scream of players.

And so, Hollywood, after all the pain and suffering, I still want to drink a toast to my abuser. I will not let them corrupt my love for you. I leave you serenading beneath your balcony, my dearest unrequited love, my maddening valentine. I will love you always and forever.

Oh, and fuck you too.

EPILOGUE

For my first month of life in Oakland, I felt as if I had just been released from prison. I attended every street fair and food festival in the whole Bay Area. I danced in the street and ate great food. I felt like my lungs hadn't tasted fresh air in a decade. I walked across the Golden Gate bridge and put my face in the bay fog like a miracle formula. Every limb and blood vessel felt cleansed.

Much to my delight, I worked almost immediately in a production of Neil Simon's *Rumors* at Center Repertory. After that, I read at Playhouse West, a Broadway caliber theatre company spearheaded by Lois Grandi, a truly gifted artistic director who was dancing professionally on Broadway at age 17. She independently created 13 full seasons of remarkable theatre in the East Bay Area. I auditioned with a monologue from *The Goodbye People* by Herb Gardner. Several years later, I was blessed to perform the entire role of Arthur in the full production which she directed. Other theatre dreams came true there as well. I had always wanted to play George in *Same Time, Next Year* by Bernard Slade. There were other lead and supporting roles in some truly great theatre pieces by writers like Jim Geoghan and Norm Foster. Altogether, I worked on stage consistently over a decade in a dozen different productions.

So, regardless of whatever I was not able to do in Hollywood, I was extraordinarily fortunate in terms of the theatre opportunities that came my way. I also at long last found local representation and several film and TV jobs. Ironically, life in the trenches of LA better positioned me for a career elsewhere. Leaving Hollywood, in my case, was the best thing I could have done for my life and career. But everyone's path takes a different course. I wish you all the luck in finding yours. Don't read too many acting books. This was the last one, ok?

Go do some acting.

DH